THE *PEARL* POEM
An Introduction and Interpretation

George Doherty Bond

Studies in Mediaeval Literature
Volume 6

The Edwin Mellen Press
Lewiston/Queenston/Lampeter

Library of Congress Cataloging-in-Publication Data

Bond, George Doherty, 1942-
   The Pearl poem : an introduction and interpretation / George D.
Bond.
     p. cm. -- (Studies in mediaeval literature ; v. 6)
    Includes bibliographical references and index.
    ISBN 0-88946-309-3
    1. Pearl (Middle English poem) 2. Christian poetry, English
(Middle)--History and criticism. I. Title. II. Series.
PR2111.B66 1990
821'.1--dc20   90-6163
                                          CIP

This is volume 6 in the continuing series
Studies in Mediaeval Literature
Volume 6 ISBN 0-88946-309-3
SML Series ISBN 0-88946-314-X

A CIP catalog record for this book
is available from the British Library.

The Edwin Mellen Press   The Edwin Mellen Press
Box 450   Box 67
Lewiston, New York   Queenston, Ontario
USA 14092   CANADA L0S 1L0

The Edwin Mellen Press, Ltd.
Lampeter, Dyfed, Wales
UNITED KINGDOM SA48 7DY

Printed in the United States of America

THE *PEARL* POEM
An Introduction and Interpretation

TABLE OF CONTENTS

ILLUSTRATIONS

ABBREVIATIONS

DNB	-	Dictionary of National Biography
EETS	-	Early English Text Society
ELH	-	English Literary History
JEGP	-	Journal of English and Germanic Philology
OED	-	Old English Dictionary, also called Oxford English Dictionary
ON	-	Old Norse
MLN	-	Modern Language Notes
MLR	-	Modern Language Review
MP	-	Modern Philology
PMLA	-	Publication of the Modern Language Association of America

PROSPECTUS

The mystery of the *Pearl*, which scholars have struggled with for 150 years, has been solved by the discovery of evidence available all the time but completely overlooked: namely, veiled allusions in the poem itself; tell-tale colors in a crude picture in the only surviving manuscript; a hidden message in two lines of innocent-looking verse; ironic entries in old chronicles of kings and queens and their loves and hates; and a revealing emblem on a fourteenth-century gravestone.

The evidence, presented in detail in Chapter IX, places the *Pearl* in a definite historic context. It identifies the characters. It names the setting.

The child in the *Pearl* is not, as scholars have supposed, an unknown poet's two-year-old daughter who appears in his strange vision as a grown woman. She is a real little girl of five, born to be a princess of England but rejected and thrust into a convent at the age of two, destroyed by sickness in childhood but raised in heaven to be a lovelier queen than any on earth.

The narrator is not a simple, private person. He is a strong, complex man facing large responsibilities, counted at the height of his career as the foremost man in England but tormented by very real failings: gross ingratitude to his benefactor, adultery of a kind specifically cursed by God, and the degradation of his own child, left unacknowledged and vulnerable.

The setting is not Paradise or fairyland. It is the kitchen garden of an old abbey in southern England, transmuted momentarily by God's light into an adjunct of heaven.

The evidence underscores the fact that the *Pearl* is not what its first editors thought it to be: a crude autobiographical poem by an amateur poet living in the childhood of the race. On the contrary, it is a work written by a man well acquainted with the learning of his day, a master of medieval veiled verse, subtle, complex, intricately beautiful. It follows a tradition, already centuries old, but revitalized and renewed by Dante.

Charged with powerful emotion, telling in vivid detail the startling, life-changing experiences of one man in one short hour, the *Pearl* dramatizes important aspects of the medieval world-view and includes a revelation of one of God's secrets, corroborated two hundred years later by the Council of Trent.

CHAPTER I

THE STRANGE HISTORY OF THE PEARL

The medieval Christian world produced not only a great body of thought but, more than that, a distinctive world-view – a mode of understanding and feeling different from both the ancient world's and the modern world's – and, to express that view, a distinctive art. The medieval view placed reality not in the sensory world, but in another world existing beyond the veil of the senses; and medieval art, aiming at effects beyond realism or classic beauty, sought to suggest unearthly light, the vast diversity of earthy phenomena held in unity by God's will, and a supersensuous beauty brighter, harder, and more splendid than reality. This art may be exemplified by the brilliant, jewel-like stained glass of the cathedral of Chartres, with its endless variety of figures and scenes, by the nave of Amiens cathedral with its soaring loveliness, and by Dante's visions of hell and heaven.

The strange and fascinating poem known today as the *Pearl* is an expression of the same force that created the medieval cathedrals and Dante's *Commedia*. Written in 1212 lines elaborately linked by rhyme and key words, it presents in taut, dramatic fashion, with bright, vivid detail, the startling, life-changing experience of one man in one short hour. As will be shown in the following chapters, it dramatizes important aspects of the medieval world-view, and its exhibits the characteristics of medieval religious poetry at its height: lavish imagery, richness of vocabulary, depth and urgency of feeling, complexity of meaning under the disguise of simplicity, and the subtlety that conceals art but challenges the reader.

All in all, the *Pearl* is the most remarkable religious poem created in medieval England, beautiful enough to have become the showpiece and epitome of an age. Nevertheless it was neglected for five centuries, was first published in the Victorian period, became briefly famous without being really read or understood, and then dropped into a welter of controversy and conflicting interpretations. This strange history can be explained, a least in part, by circumstances.

As will be shown later, the story of the *Pearl* is based on an experience of Henry, 3rd Earl of Lancaster, in August, 1311, or some closely successive year, but the poem was commissioned and written later, most likely in the 1360's and perhaps not completed until 1370 or a little later. The patron and sponsor of the poem was probably Henry's son, the 1st Duke of Lancaster, or his granddaughter Blanche, who became the Duchess of Lancaster. Both died in outbreaks of the Black Death, the Duke in 1361, the Duchess in 1369. Their deaths probably deprived the poem of the brilliant introduction to society they could have provided.

Other circumstances of time and change also affected the *Pearl*. Between 1378 and 1417 the medieval religious faith, already weakened by earlier attacks, was shaken by the Great Schism, which split the Christian world into two parts, each supporting a different Pope; and this crisis facilitated the development in England of a new secular outlook and a new literature, exemplified by Chaucer's works. In this environment the *Pearl* found no place. Furthermore, all too quickly the western dialect in which it was written ceased to be a viable literary language.

The world that created the cathedrals and Dante and the *Pearl* came to an end in the struggles that produced the modern world; and the new men – the Renaissance men – turned their backs on all things medieval and set out to create a new civilization based on the validity of the senses, the discovery and formulation of the laws of nature through accurate observation, and faith in man. For inspiration and guidance they turned to the Greek and Roman classics; they accepted the Greek concept of art as representation; and they eagerly embraced the classic ideals of order, harmony, and the golden mean. Feeling only contempt for medieval thought and art, they rejected even the most beautiful expressions of the medieval mind. Dante's *Commedia*, they felt, was "tainted by a barbaric spirit," and the art of the cathedrals was debased. The phrase "the barbarous Gothic style" (applied to the cathedrals) was repeated so often it became a cliché.[1]

In seventeenth-century England it came to be the general opinion that the medieval period had been an age of "grosenesse and barbarousnesse" in which "al good letters were almost asleepe." Protestant theologians labeled it as a period of "doctrinal deformity" and rejected it from consideration. Scholars found so little value in its literature that they concluded English poetry might be said to have originated with the Elizabethans.[2]

Medieval buildings, records, and manuscripts were allowed to fall into decay, and in some instances castles and abbeys were actually quarried for building stone. Thousands of manuscripts were lost or destroyed. That medieval manuscripts were preserved at all is due primarily to a succession of antiquarians and collectors such as Archbishop Parker, John Leland, Sir Thomas Bodley, William Camden, Sir William Dugdale, and Sir Robert Cotton and his son and grandson.

From the general destruction visited upon medieval artifacts the *Pearl* emerged in a single, handwritten copy, without title, author's name, scribe's name, or any other identification, in a manuscript prepared about the year 1400, which also contained three other untitled, unidentified poems in the same dialect. This MS. belonged in the early 1600's to Henry Savile, of Banke, Yorkshire, and passed from his hands to those of Sir Robert Cotton.[3] With the rest of the Cotton collection it became the property of the English government in 1700 and was given a permanent home in the British Museum in 1753. At an unknown time it was bound with other medieval writings, the whole being catalogued under a single number as MS Cotton Nero A x.

Nothing is known about the early history of the manuscript other than the facts given above. Possibly it went unread from Renaissance days to the eighteenth century, for no one in those days felt much interest in medieval poetry (except that of Chaucer and his school) and the reading of it for idle entertainment would be discouraged by the difficult handwriting, the unidentified dialect, and the many rare words. James, Sir Robert Cotton's librarian, apparently did little more than look at the first few pages; at any rate his classification of the contents as "an old poem in English in which under the figment of a dream, many things relating to religion and morals are explained" (Vetus poema Anglicanum, in quo sub insomnii figmento multa ad religionem et mores spectantia explicantur)[4] clearly indicates he had not read far enough to discover that the manuscript contained more than one poem. A later librarian, Thomas Smith, in his catalogue merely repeated in paraphrase what James had written.

In the second half of the eighteenth century, for the first time, there came a great stirring of interest in the Middle Ages. Men and women, reacting against rationalism and tedium, found mysterious beauty in "Gothic ruins" and adventure in tales of knighthood.

At this time Thomas Warton, poet and Oxford professor, while gathering material for his *History of English Poetry* (3 vols; 1774-1781), looked into MS Cotton Nero A x and read far enough to see that it contained at least two poems. Of the first (the *Pearl*) he wrote:

A Vision on vellum, perhaps of the same age [i.e., the reign of Edward III, 1327-1377] is alliterative.

He then quoted fourteen lines.[5] Thus the *Pearl* made its unheralded entry into English literary history four hundred years after it was written.

In the first half of the nineteenth century interest in medieval life and literature was augmented by interest in the history of the English language and its various dialects. About 1830 Richard Price, employed to edit a new edition of Warton's *History*, and Frederic Madden, Keeper of Manuscripts in the British Museum, each chanced upon the last poem in MS Cotton Nero A x, a story of Sir Gawain, and each determined to publish it. About the same time Guest, working on a history of English metrics, looked into the manuscript and conjectured that the poems were in the Scottish dialect and were written by Huchoun of the Awle Ryal, a Scottish poet mentioned by an early chronicler.[6] Price died before he could carry out his resolve, but Madden published the poem in 1839, giving it the title "Syr Gawayne and the Grene Kni3ht."

In the course of preparing the text for publication Madden read the entire manuscript and became the first to point out that it contained four poems and to describe the contents of each. Though recognizing that the dialect was not Scottish, he accepted the idea that they were written by a Scot and suggested that the manuscript had been copied and its language altered by "a scribe of the Midland counties." Thus the ground was prepared for a scholarly argument that drew further attention to the manuscript.

Madden's summary of the *Pearl* constitutes the first recorded attempt of a modern reader to interpret the content of the poem. It reads as follows:

> The writer represents himself as going in the month of August to seek his *pearl* or mistress, and falling asleep in a flowery arbour. He is carried in his vision to a stream near a forest, which flows over pebbles of emeralds and sapphires. On the other side he perceives a chrystal [sic] cliff, and "a mayden of menske" sitting beneath....The lady rises and approaches him, and in answer to his inquiries blames him for supposing her lost. He wishes to pass the stream, but is told he may not till after death. The lady thence takes occasion to instruct him in religious doctrines, which are of a mystical tendency. The celestial Jerusalem is then pointed out to him, and he beholds a procession of virgins going to salute the Lamb. The lady leaves him to take her place among them; and on his attempting to jump into the stream to follow her, he awakes.[7]

This summary launched the *Pearl* on its long course of confusion and misinterpretation. First, it virtually ignores the content of two thirds of the poem, including the whole central section. Second, it presents some hasty guesses as facts; for example, that the "I" of the poem was the author and that the child portrayed was the author's mistress.

Nobody called attention to these errors at the time, but the linguists (then called philologists) took note of Madden's comments about the language.

In 1864, when the Early English Text Society was organized, its first project was publication of the three unpublished poems in MS Cotton Nero A x; and the laborious task of transcribing them, letter by letter, was entrusted to Richard Morris, one of the Society's founders. He performed this service well, also dealing masterfully with the questions about the dialect. His conclusion was that they had been written in the West Midland dialect of the fourteenth century and that "the uniformity and consistency of the grammatical forms" proved they had not been transcribed from any other dialect. Modern linguistic science confirms his verdict.

With regard to his handling of the content of the manuscript, his work was not so commendable. Like most Victorian scholars, he retained the prejudices against medieval things inherited from earlier generations; and these prejudices blinded him to the real qualities of the *Pearl* and the other two poems. To him they were "treatises," each written "for the purpose of enforcing, by line upon line and precept upon precept" some moral or religious commonplace. The *Pearl*, he said succinctly, enforces "Resignation to the will of God" while at the same time expressing the author's "own sorrow for the loss of his infant child, a girl of two years old."[8]

Thus, without mentioning any discrepancy between his and Madden's interpretations, Morris followed Madden's example and presented his assumptions as facts. With complete assurance he disregarded (or perhaps never saw) the possibility that the *Pearl* might possess any subtlety, ambiguity, depth, or shade of meaning not obvious to him. For example, like Madden, he assumed that the "I" of the poem was the author. How did he know? He never said. Probably what lay behind his certainty was simply the general belief in the childish naivete of medieval men. Since the poem begins with "I" talking, "I" was bound to be the author, for no one in the Middle Ages was far enough advanced to think of using it in any other way. Furthermore, on the basis of his positive interpretation of one ambiguous phrase, he concluded that the child of the poem had died before she was two, even though she is portrayed as an older child. Again, the discrepancy – the obvious gap between the child's age and the child's looks and behavior – required no comment; it was merely further evidence of medieval lack of critical and artistic standards.

Morris's concept of the *Pearl* was fully acceptable to scholars of his day. Furthermore it held elements of popular appeal to the Victorian reading public, which relished well-turned moral lessons and doted on sob-stories. Bernhard ten Brink, a professor at the University of Strasbourg, saw the possibilities and laid hold of them manfully in the first volume of his history of English literature (published 1877, translated into English 1883). Undeterred by lack of facts, he composed an imaginary biography of the author of the *Pearl*:

The poet has married (his lord having, perhaps, given
him a home of his own as a reward for faithful service). A
child, a sweet girl, radiant in innocence, had blessed his union.
The father concentrated all his affection upon the child, and so
exclusively that we are led to believe the mother had not long
survived her birth. The dearest ideals of the thoughtful poet
were embodied in his daughter. But the pitiless hand of fate
tore her away at the tenderest age. The poem describes the
father's feelings at her death, and tells how he was comforted.[9]

At this time, encouraged by the progress in linguistic studies,
numerous scholars in Britain and elsewhere were envisioning a literary
science that would include both language and literature and would take its
place beside the natural sciences as one of the great branches of knowledge.
By means of this new science they expected to be able to establish the
pedigree of any given manuscript and its exact relationship to the author's
original composition, to classify genres of literature with precision, and to
identify and define literary conventions so accurately that the conventional
and the original elements in works of art could be pinpointed.

In general scholars of this time gave a scientific cast to their inherited
prejudice against medieval literature by making its "crudeness" or
"barbarousness" the result of the stage of society it represented. For
example, the miracle plays were crude because they belonged to "the actual
childhood of the drama." On the other hand, the Victorian period, in which
these scholars grew to manhood, was, in their estimation, obviously mature;
so they could judge correctly the qualities of literature created on a lower
level of civilization. Thus they established the "scientific" doctrine of the
evolution of literature – the idea that for each new type or form of literature
there must be a small beginning and a gradual growth from generation to
generation. The theory was stated by Courthope as follows:

Movement in political history is measured by the achievements
of arms and commerce; in constitutional history by changes in
laws and institutions, by the spectacle of

Freedom slowly broadening down
From precedent to precedent;

in poetry, and the other arts of expression, it is manifested by
the simultaneous appearance in the nation of new modes of
thought, fresh modes of composition, improved methods of
harmony. Mind works upon mind; the small beginnings of one
generation are carried forward, if only a little way, in the next.

Hence we cannot afford to despise the rude art of our forefathers....[10]

"The rude art of our forefathers!" With that predetermined judgment no one was likely to look with insight or understanding into an earlier art or literature that followed standards different from those of his own day. Unfortunately these scholars gave no thought to the fact that the evolution of literature exists in a "timeless present" and that great models were available to the fourteenth century as well as to the Victorians.

The next contributor to the misinterpretation of the *Pearl* was Israel Gollancz, a Cambridge graduate, beginning in 1890 a long and productive career as scholar and teacher. Inspired both by ten Brink's imaginary biography of the *Pearl's* author and by the ideas and goals of the new literary science, he resolved to publish the *Pearl* in a form that would reach out "far beyond the limited circle of students of Middle English" to the general public as well as to all English teachers in school and college.

With great fervor and ability he carried the project to completion. He translated the *Pearl*, as he understood it, into poetic-sounding Victorian speech, plentifully sprinkled with archaisms such as *wot, trow, doth*, and *ne'er*. He courted and won powerful backers. From the Laureate (Lord Tennyson) he obtained a quatrain hailing his effort to reset the *Pearl* "in Britain's lyric coronet." This he displayed in capitals on an otherwise bare page. From "the greatest of modern Pre-Raphaelites" (W. Holman Hunt) he procured a portrait of the child in the *Pearl* (pictured as a pained-looking woman of twenty or older), and this he used as a frontispiece.

To introduce the poem, he wrote a masterly introduction. The *Pearl*, he said, is an "early *In Memoriam*" (one of Queen Victoria's favorite poems), and it occupies a "peculiar position" in the evolution of English poetry. It is, in fact, an evolutionary link between the earlier poets "whose literary ancestors were Caedmon and Cynewulf" and the newer poets (like Chaucer). Furthermore, it not only antedates "Chaucer's first ambitious effort, 'The Book of the Duchess,'" but also surpasses it "not only by its intrinsic beauty, but even more by its simple and direct appeal to what is eternal and elemental in human nature."

Having satisfied the need for a scientific approach, Gollancz went on to satisfy equally well the Victorian taste for sentiment and pathos. To ten Brink's imaginary biography of the poet he added five pages of further "hypothetical" details. A few samples are quoted below:

> Two or three years before the date of 'Gawain' the poet had married; his wedded life was unhappy; the idealised object of his love had disappointed him, and it is to be feared had proved unfaithful...[Gollancz assumed not only that "I" of the *Pearl* wrote all four poems in MS Cotton Nero A x but also that he wrote them in a particular order, *Sir Gawain and the Green Knight* being the first.]
> 'Gawain' is the story of a noble knight triumphing over sore temptations that beset his vows of chastity. How often, while drawing this ideal picture, did the poet's thoughts recur to the saddest reality of his own life! ...
> Yet his wedded life had brought him one great happiness – an only child, a daughter, on whom he lavished all the wealth of his love and tenderness. He named the child 'Marjory' or 'Marguerite'; she was his 'pearl,' – his emblem of holiness and innocence. But his happiness was shortlived; before two years had passed the poet's home was desolate.

All this he put into a handsome, gilt-edge volume, with his translation and the text of the poem on alternate pages, and dedicated the whole "To A CHILD'S Love" [his capitals].[11]

In this guise the *Pearl* went out over the English-speaking world and won a kind of fame. Since the story, as Gollancz and Morris conceived it, was in the first few stanzas and the last few, readers could look at those quickly, compare the translation with the queer-looking words on the opposite page, and feel satisfied they had the whole meaning. Even George Saintsbury, who should have known better, was hypnotized by Gollancz's creation and thought he heard the "melancholy clangour" of the rhymes in the original. Within a few years the story of the poet and his beloved daughter was incorporated into so many college lectures, textbooks, histories of English literature, and encyclopedias that it became as familiar as something in the Bible or Shakespeare.

Inevitably, as knowledge and understanding of medieval literature increased, dissent arose. In 1904, after a dozen years of uncontested acceptance, Gollancz's interpretation of the *Pearl* was called in question by two Americans, representing the rising universities of America and the young but powerful Modern Language Association, in a single issue of whose *Publication* they were allowed a total of 100 pages for presentation of their views.

One of the Americans, Carleton Brown, addressed himself to showing that the Gollancz interpretation neglected the central meaning of the *Pearl*. Lines 421-719, he said, contain "nothing more or less than a sustained theological argument," and lines 600-743 contain the "the real climax of the poem." The *Pearl*, he concluded, is a serious poem dealing with certain religious ideas at issue in the fourteenth century.[12]

The other American, W. H. Schofield of Harvard, made a scatter-gun attack on the whole Morris/ten Brink/Gollancz interpretation. He poured scorn on the inventors of hypothetical biographies and on those who quote such biographies as fact. He pointed out that the poem nowhere says that the narrator was the child's father and emphatically asserted that the poem is not "in the least elegiac or autobiographical," but is, instead, "obviously a vision," in which the opposing religious views of the narrator and the child are presented in the style of a medieval literary "debate." To illustrate his point, he cited a variety of medieval poems (including *Piers Plowman* and the *Roman de la Rose*) which show a vision used as a setting for "didactic allegory." He also stressed the obvious but hitherto disregarded fact that the child of the poem does not dress, talk, or behave like a two-year-old and drew the conclusion that she was not intended to be taken as a real child. Instead, he said, she was clearly intended as a personification of Pure Maidenhood.

At the end of this sweeping attack, in embarrassing disregard of all he had previously said, he added a hasty postscript to the effect that Professor E. K. Rand had just pointed out to him the real source of the *Pearl*: Boccaccio's 14th Eclogue, in which the author of the *Decameron* tells of seeing and talking with his dead daughter. Thus Schofield scuttled his own argument and left only the general impression that he thought the Morris/ten Brink/Gollancz interpretation was wrong no matter how you looked at it.[13]

There were personal dignities at stake and vested interests to protect. Though Brown's article might be ignored, Schofield's sharply worded attack could not be. So a champion of the accepted view was needed. G. G. Coulton, historian and controversialist, also a Cambridge man, then busy on a rhymed translation of the *Pearl*, accepted the role. Since Schofield had used sarcasm, he replied in the same vein. He did not choose to defend Gollancz or any other aggrieved person – no, he chose, rather, to defend the *Pearl*. If the child in the poem was merely a personification of Pure Maidenhood, he asked derisively, "how could the author's lost maidenhood now be safe in heaven (lines 257ff.)? ... Our imagination staggers," he continued, "at the gulf between what the author actually wrote and what his critic imagines him to have written." In short, he concludes, "I cannot help thinking that the demonstrably false conception of medieval life from which Professor Schofield starts supplies the key to his heterodoxy, and that our rude forefathers who took *Pearl* for an elegy have not erred at all."[14] (At this point a modern reader may feel some doubt about the reliability of Coulton's rhetorical assurance; for which if any of our ancestors read the *Pearl* before Warton in 1744 and whether or not they were "rude" and whether they took it for an elegy, neither Coulton nor anyone else had any way of knowing.)

Thus Schofield was publicly chastised, and notice was served on all that the Morris/ten Brink/Gollancz interpretation was correct and final and that any deviation from it would be punished.

The results were drastic. Schofield apologized lamely in 1909,[15] and further dissent was inhibited for a decade. When it did reappear in 1918, it was offered in a muted way. Without criticizing any other view, without even making clear the relation of his interpretation to the prevailing one, R. M. Garrett of the University of Washington offered a paean of praise to the "flawlessness" of the *Pearl* and, in connection with extensive citations and quotes bearing on the importance and inner meaning of the Eucharist in the fourteenth century, the prominence of pearls in the New Testament, and the symbolic connection of the pearl with the Eucharist in patristic literature, he suggested that the *Pearl* "has as its central idea the fundamental teachings of the Eucharist." The presentation is curiously indirect, as though he hoped to evade the unfriendly guardians of the *Pearl*, offer his private insight to other scholars, and slip back into the shadows before anyone could collar him or argue with him.[16] His monograph attracted little attention, none of it favorable. Even Carleton Brown chided him.[17]

The treatment of Garrett's proposal offered no encouragement to dissenters. Nevertheless other dissents were registered in the 1920's. In a short article W. K. Greene, soon to become a dean at Duke University, interpreted the *Pearl* as a parable, that is, a piece of fiction invented for the purpose of conveying a truth. Thus, in his view, the man and child of the poem were not the poet and his daughter but, rather, fictional characters created by an unknown poet.[18] In the second dissent, a book-length study, Sister Mary Madeleva examined the *Pearl* in comparison with the works of medieval mystics such as Angelo of Foligno, Gertrude the Great, Juliana of Norwich, and Ramon Lull. Like Schofield, she interpreted the poem as an allegory; but, unlike him, she took the narrator to be a religious and the child to be his soul. The *Pearl*, she concluded, is the spiritual autobiography of a religious.[19]

In a third dissent, Oscar Cargill and Margaret Schlauch proposed the identification (without any real evidence) of the child as Margaret, one of Edward III's granddaughters who died at the age of two. In an offhand way they also suggested the application to the *Pearl* of the medieval concept of four levels of meaning.[20]

Obviously all these proposals went off in different directions; and to the holders of the orthodox view they no doubt seemed unintelligible or perverse. So they could conveniently be ignored.

Meanwhile Gollancz worked industriously to strengthen his position. In the *Cambridge History of English Literature* (Vol. I, 1907) in a magisterial chapter of four poems in MS Cotton Nero A x he restated his view of the *Pearl*, including his imaginary biography of the author. In 1910, for the *Encyclopaedia Britannica*, he summarized what he had said in that chapter. In 1918 he published a revised translation of the *Pearl*, and in 1921 a new, augmented edition of the poem, including in an appendix the Latin text and a translation of Boccaccio's 14th Eclogue, which, he concluded, bore no demonstrable relationship to the *Pearl*.[21] During the same period he also prepared and published editions of the other three poems in MS Cotton

Nero A x, and in 1923 a facsimile reproduction of the entire manuscript.[22] He was knighted in 1919 and died in 1930.

Even after his death his views continued to dominate. His chapter in the *Cambridge History*, present in every university library, emanated authority. His article in the *Britannica*, repeated in every edition and every printing from 1910 to 1960, signed by Gollancz, quoting what Gollancz said in the *Cambridge History*, and, after 1928, citing in its bibliography only books written or edited by Gollancz, bore constant witness that nothing should be added to or taken away from what Gollancz had said.

The preemption of the *Pearl* by Gollancz and his followers not only discouraged new studies; it also tended to prevent or slow any reshaping of the scholarly view of the poem as new knowledge accumulated. Osgood, first American editor of the *Pearl* (1906), saw the poem as far more complex and beautiful than Gollancz did, but his views were disregarded.[23] J. B. Fletcher, Dante scholar, writing in 1921, quietly demonstrated, by placing quotations from the *Pearl* side by side with quotations from medieval religious writings, that the author of the *Pearl* painted the portrait of "his glorified maiden" in the very colors of the symbolic portraits of the Virgin Mary and that he consciously and deftly made use of many-faceted symbols. If these points are correct, he continued, the question, "Is the story of the *Pearl* literally true, or is the child a personification of something" is "an altogether false dilemma." The child "may have really lived and died; she may have been the poet's own daughter," but those facts would not keep her from also symbolizing Innocence in one connection and the Virgin in another. For, though the personifications of some medieval writers (following classical models, like Boethius' *Consolation of Philosophy*) have a single fixed reference and one meaning only, the symbols of the religious writers have multiple references and many meanings.[24] His wise words went largely unheeded.

The first new study to achieve a degree of acceptance appeared in 1933, the work of René Wellek, then at Charles University, in Prague. He accepted the orthodox identification of the narrator and child, but saw clearly that "the purely elegiac interpretation" (which Gollancz had insisted upon) made the poem "an unartistic conglomerate." In Carleton Brown's article, he said, for the first time the contents of the poem were taken seriously enough to permit an investigation "at its very center, the theological discussion, no longer regarded as a mere digression." To the aesthetic qualities of the *Pearl* he responded almost as enthusiastically as Garrett and Fletcher, and described eloquently "its finished grace, the unearthly loveliness of its descriptions, the heavy brocade of its strange diction."[25]

E. V. Gordon of Oxford University, working in the 1930's on a new edition of the *Pearl*, agreed ostensibly with Wellek on the beauty and artistry of the *Pearl* but also maintained the older and contradictory view that the poem showed incomplete artistic control and contained botched details and invented or distorted words. Thus he did not present a coherent view. Nevertheless his book, first published in 1953, long after his death, with revisions by his wife, is notable for the excellence of its text (he removed many of Gollancz's fanciful emendations), its valuable notes, and its carefully researched glossary.[26]

Between 1933 and 1965 six more dissenting voices were raised. D. W. Robertson, of Princeton, and Milton R. Stern offered conflicting analyses of different levels of meaning in the *Pearl*.[27] Sister Mary Vincent Hillman, John Allen Conley, and Marie Hamilton proposed new allegorical interpretations.[28] Mother Angela Carson suggested that the child in the *Pearl* was really a girl from a foreign country with whom the poet had fallen in love, thus returning full-cycle to the first interpretation, that by Frederic Madden.[29]

Around 1960 a shift in attitude toward the *Pearl* became evident. The *Britannica* dropped Gollancz's article, relegating the *Pearl* to a brief mention in the section on English literature. A French critic, with Gallic wit, graciously granted to every reader the right to interpret the poem in any way he liked.[30] A famous linguistic scholar scored the exponents of four-level interpretations for applying a system without any "criteria of corrigibility."[31] Various scholars, in varied ways, pronounced the meaning of the poem a mystery beyond solution.[32]

Despite the frustration and disappointment shown, a large advance in understanding the *Pearl* had resulted from the long clash of views. Nobody believed any longer that the *Pearl* was simple, direct, and crude. On the contrary both the orthodox and the dissenters had found it to be complex in meaning, subtle in thought, and beautifully intricate in workmanship.

Many barriers to understanding still existed: our natural tendency to see only what our world-view recognizes, some of Morris's initial assumptions, never tested for validity, still blocking the way; an unfortunate propensity of earlier scholars to obtain a desired reading by emending or disregarding particular passages because they were "conventional," or contained "botched details," or used words merely for rhyme or alliteration, or by interpreting a passage, not by what is said, but by what some medieval writer had said somewhere; and, lastly, the common practice, among both the orthodox and the dissenters, of strongly asserting a notion without bothering about the lack of evidence or of any guide or criterion by which the claim could be tested.

But these are not insuperable obstacles. Twentieth-century scholarship has amassed a tremendous amount of medieval research, and it is not lacking in material bearing on the "cultural movement which tended to fuse the two currents of courtly, chivalric love with philosophical, spiritual or divine love,"[33] as in Dante and the *Pearl*, and the related flowering of religious poetry in the thirteenth and fourteenth centuries.

The breakthrough in understanding the *Pearl*, presented below and long overdue, has come through painstaking re-examination of the poem (along with Morris' assumptions) in the light of the following premises:

1. The *Pearl* dramatizes ideas of great importance to the medieval world-view.

2. It follows a medieval theory of poetry different from the modern theory.

3. It can and should be interpreted in accordance with the guide to this kind of poetry prepared about 1306 by Dante, speaking both as poet and scholar.

When so examined, the dramatic story of the man and the child becomes much more definite and understandable. Then, with the help of evidence from the manuscript and contemporary chronicles, identification of the characters becomes possible.

Chapter I
Endnotes

1. Angelina La Piana, *Dante's American Pilgrimage* (New Haven: Yale University Press, 1948), p. 17.

2. *Ibid.*, p. 13.

3. *Pearl*, ed. Sir Israel Gollancz (London, 1921, rpt. New York: Cooper Square Publishers, 1906), p. xiv.

4. *Ibid.*, p. xiv.

5. *The History of English Poetry*, ed. Richard Price (London, 1824), III, 393.

6. Syr Gawayne: *A Collection of Ancient Romance Poems*, ed. with introduction, notes and glossary, by Sir Frederick Madden (London, 1839; rptd. New York: AMS Press, 1977), pp. 299-304.

7. *Ibid.*, pp. xlviii-ix.

8. *Early English Alliterative Poems in the West Midland Dialect*, EETS, O. S. 1 (London, 1864; 1969), p. 14.

9. *Early English Literature (to Wiclif)*, tr. Horace M. Kennedy (New York: Henry Holt, 1883), p. 348.

10. W. J. Courthope, *A History of English Poetry* (6 vols. London, 1895; rptd. London and New York: Macmillan, 1919), I, xv.

11. *Pearl*, ed. with Modern Rendering by Israel Gollancz (London: David Nutt, 1891).

12. C. F. Brown, "The Author of *The Pearl* Considered in the Light of His Theological Opinions," PMLA 19 (1904), 115-153.

13. W. H. Schofield, "The Nature and Fabric of *The Pearl*," PMLA 19 (1904), 154-215.

14. G. G. Coulton, "In Defence of *Pearl*," MLR 2 (1906), 39-43.

15. Schofield, "Symbolism, Allegory, and Autobiography in *The Pearl*," PMLA 24 (1909), 639.

16. Robert Max Garrett, "*The Pearl*: An Interpretation," *University of Washington Publications in English* 4 (1918), 1-45.

17. Brown, MLN 34 (1919), 42-45.

18. Walter Kirkland Greene, "*The Pearl*-A New Interpretation," PMLA 40 (1925), 814-827.

19. Sister M. Madeleva, *Pearl: A Study in Spiritual Dryness* (New York: D. Appleton & Co., 1925; rptd. Phaeton Press, 1968).

20. O. Cargill and M. Schlauch, "*The Pearl* and Its Jeweller," PMLA 43 (1928), 105-123.

21. *Pearl*, ed. I. Gollancz, (London, 1921; rptd. New York: Cooper Square Publishers, Inc., 1966), p. 244.
    David Carlson in a more recent argument convincingly demonstrates that "the contention that the Pearl poet knew Olympia is unproven....The limited circulation of the Buccolium Carmen...and the histories and natures of the two manuscripts of it that later leave Italy militate against the internal evidence that Pearl - poet used Boccacio's *Olympia*" (186).

22. *Cleanness* (London, Part I, 1921); *Patience* (1913; 2nd ed., 1924); *Sir Gawain and the Green Knight* (1912); and *Pearl, Cleanness, Patience, and Sir Gawain*, reproduced in facsimile from the unique MS Cotton Nero A x in the British Museum, with introduction by Sir I. Gollancz; EETS, O. S. 162 (London, 1923).

23. *The Pearl: A Middle English Poem*, ed. Charles G. Osgood (Boston: D. C. Heath, 1906).

24. Jefferson B. Fletcher, "The Allegory of the Pearl," JEGP 20 (1921), 1-21. Several more recent critics have pointed out that the opposition between allegorical and elegiac readings poses a false dilemma. Stephen Russell, for instance, sees the poem as moving developmentally: "I can see the poem as profoundly and radically developmental and see the image of the pearl as an emblem of this development from elegy to Christian didacticism." Davenport states "They [the Dreamer and the Maiden] both are and are not allegorical; the experience of the poem is both real and unreal." (37).

25. René Wellek, "The Pearl: An Interpretation of the Middle English Poem," *Studies in English 4* (Prague: Charles University, 1933), 5-33.

26. *Pearl*, ed. E. V. Gordon (Oxford: Clarendon Press, 1953).

27. D. W. Robertson, Jr., "The Pearl as a Symbol," MLN, 65 (1950) 155-161; Milton R. Stern, "An Approach to the *The Pearl*," JEGP 54 (1955), 684-692.

28. Sister Mary Vincent Hillman, "Some Debatable Words In *Pearl* and Its Theme," MLN 60 (1945), 241-248; John Allen Conley, "*Pearl* and a Lost Tradition," JEGP 54 (1955), 332-347; Marie Padgett Hamilton, "The Meaning of the Middle English *Pearl*," PMLA 70 (1955), 805-824.

18

29. Mother Angela Carson, O. S. U., "Aspects of Elegy in the Middle English *Pearl*," SP 62 (1965), 17-17.

30. Fernand Mosse, *A Handbook of Middle English*, tr. James A. Walker (Baltimore: Johns Hopkins Press, 1952), p. 248.

31. Morton W. Bloomfield, "Symbolism in Medieval Literature," MP 56 (November, 1958), 80.

32. A. R. Heiserman, "The Plot of 'Pearl,'" PMLA 80 (June, 1965), 171; Dorothy Everett, *Essays on Middle English Literature* (Oxford: Clarendon Press, 1955), p. 94.

33. Dante Alighiere, *The Divine Comedy*, tr. in prose with introduction and notes by H. R. Huse (New York: Rinehart, 1954), pp. iii-iv.

CHAPTER II

IDEAS WONDROUSLY EMBODIED

The Victorian interpreters of the *Pearl*, being products of the Renaissance, the Enlightenment, and the Age of Science, saw little or nothing that an intelligent person could accept in the religious ideas of the Middle Ages, sometimes called the Age of Faith. We also, being products of the same forces, have difficulty with these ideas, for the world-view then accepted runs counter to many of our concepts and prejudices.

As moderns, we believe in the truth of science and relate all other knowledge to scientific fact; but educated medieval men believed in the truth of theology and related all other knowledge to that. As modern men, we see an orderly world of natural phenomena governed by scientific law; but medieval men saw an unstable and unpredictable world governed by the direct working of God's will. We seek truth in objective study and test all ideas and hypotheses against fact and factual experience; educated medieval men, on the other hand, thought fact to be superficial and tried to see through and beyond it to God's meaning. In their view every visible thing was a theophany or appearance of God, and the highest intellectual process was contemplation, i.e., the raising of the mind above the factual to the real. Thus the medieval world placed a far higher value on insight, intuition, pure intellect, than we do. To Dante, for example, God himself is intellect, and the supreme faculty of man's soul is mind, which "participates in the divine nature under the aspect of everlasting intelligence."[1]

Because we believe in the life of the senses, we seek happiness on earth; but medieval men, always aware of filth, disease, pain, and death, sought happiness elsewhere. We think of eternity – if we think of it at all – as an endless succession of moments or years; but medieval thought conceived of it in more than one way – sometimes as we do, sometimes as an everpresent timelessness enclosing present, past, and future in one changeless totality. We have no clear idea of heaven; but medieval men knew it to be everything that earth is not: pure, eternal, shining, inexpressibly beautiful, free from all shadow, boredom, and pain. We make of our worship little more than a passive participation in a public service; but medieval man came to his church to make contact with God and his loved ones beyond the veil.

To many of us the sacraments – baptism and the Eucharist – are symbols and reminders; but to medieval men they were mysteries, sources of power – not only symbols but potent and perfected means of linking men with God and gaining his favor.

These ideas, which helped to create the distinctive character of the Middle Ages, were already under attack when the fourteenth century opened. Duns Scotus by means of subtle objections and reservations was weakening the foundations, and within a few decades William of Ockham and Marsiglio of Padua were busily engaged in undermining the whole structure. The Popes, in their captivity at Avignon, were hard put to hold the Church together; and one of them, John XXII, was himself surrounded by controversy and dissension. Even the beholders of heavenly visions – for example, Meister Eckhart and Dante – were likely to find themselves in collision both with the Church and with those who were attacking Church doctrines.

The Pearl, born into this world of controversy after the middle of the century, makes no direct reference to any controversy of the time; but dramatically, through the words of its characters, and, even more dramatically, through the scenes and events portrayed, it centers attention on matters at issue in that day.

The religious ideas argued by the man and the child have been noted and discussed by students of the *Pearl*. For instance, the man objects to the idea that the child has become a Queen in heaven, and the child seeks to enlighten him by retelling (lines 501-572) the Parable of the Vineyard from Matthew 20. In the parable, she explains, each laborer received the same pay, no matter whether he had worked all day or only a few minutes; and likewise she, though she had died young without doing much work in God's vineyard, had received the same reward as those who had labored long for God. When the man objects to her answer, on the grounds that men should be rewarded in accordance with their good works, she makes plain that no man is good enough to make any claim against God and that men reach heaven only through God's grace. Thus she counters a view current at Oxford University at one period in the fourteenth century, according to Bishop (later Archbishop) Bradwardine,[2] and upholds the teaching of the Church. In doing so, she does not, as Carleton Brown accused her of doing, support the idea of equal reward in heaven. She shows (445-456) that though all who enter the "cort of þe kyndom of God" are kings and queens, nevertheless there are ranks in heaven. Her answer involves the paradox of superiority on the one hand but no inferiority on the other. It is the same paradox treated by Dante (cf. *Paradiso*, iii, 88-90)[3] and sometimes explained this way: every saved soul receives the same gift from God, but different souls have differing abilities to perceive and use the gift.[3a]

The child also gives strong statements on the nature and power of the sacraments of baptism and the Eucharist. The water of baptism is the water that came from Jesus' side when the spear was thrust into his body on the cross, and this water washes away the sins in which Adam plunged all of us. The rich blood from his side is the wine of the sacraments (implied 646-656, 1207-1210) that saves us from hell and "þe deth secounde."

In upholding the salvation of baptized children who died before reaching the age of accountability, the poem is also dealing with a point that had long been in question. The Church Fathers expressed contradictory opinions on it; and Pope Innocent III, after considering the matter, declined to pronounce a decision.[4] However, in 1311, at the Council of Vienne, Pope Clement V held in favor of their salvation.[5] The *Pearl*, through the witness of a child in heaven (625-636), corroborates Clement's decision.

The religious ideas dramatized in the poem but not directly discussed have received much less attention from scholars, and some of them have scarcely been recognized as ideas or as being worth discussing. Yet their embodiment in narration or description shows they had importance to the author, and their vividness in presentation may actually make them more impressive to a responsive reader than the ideas that are merely discussed.

One such idea is that miracles happen. Thus, for the narrator, while his body lies in a trance on the mound where he lost his pearl, the sky splits open, God's light streams down, and all things are changed. The gravel beneath his feet becomes oriental pearls, and the pebbles in the nearby stream become emeralds, sapphires, and other gems. (The fact that some have taken this picture to be conventional, a representation of fairyland or the earthly paradise, is a measure of their distance from the world of ideas that prevailed in the Middle Ages.) Near the end of the poem the narrator is permitted to see the City of God, the New Jerusalem. It descends through the air and he is permitted to look into its streets and buildings. Thus is dramatized the fact that a living man, even a sinner like the narrator of the *Pearl*, may through God's grace see heaven. The high Middle Ages never doubted this, and visions of heaven and hell were frequent and everywhere accepted, but by the 1380's ideas had changed so much that Chaucer was able to deny the possibility of any man of his day seeing such a vision:

> A thousand sythes have I herd men telle
> That there is joye in hevene and peyne in helle,
> And I accorde wel that it be so;
> But natheles, this wot I wel also,
> That there ne is non that dwelleth in this countre,
> That eyther hath in helle or hevene ybe,
> Ne may of it no other weyes witen,
> But as he hath herd seyd or founde it writen; ...[6]

Another idea that is dramatically presented is the coexistence of eternity and time, and the unchanging nature of heaven. The city the narrator describes is the same city that Saint John saw and described in Revelation 21.10-23: it is a great walled city, built upon a foundation of twelve huge precious stones, with twelve gates, each consisting of a single pearl. Some of the details the narrator gives may seem to alter or contradict the Biblical account: the twelve layers of stone that constitute the foundation are arranged in the form of twelve steep, broad steps (this stair-step arrangement is not mentioned by St. John) and the varied colors of the steps are noted: the first is green jasper; the third is pearly pale chalcedony; the eighth is clear, white beryl; the ninth is twin-hued topaz; the twelfth is amethyst, purple blended with blue (no colors are specifically mentioned by St. John). Furthermore, the walls and buildings of the city are transparent (St. John says only that the wall was of jasper and "the city was pure gold, like unto pure glass"), and the interiors of the buildings, visible through the transparent materials, are ornamented with jewels and precious stones (these details are not given by St. John). Last, the gates are open and unguarded (in St. John's account an angel stands at each gate).

The total effect seems very different from that given in Revelation: the city of the *Pearl* suggests a medieval stronghold, built high upon a foundation of rock, but this account neither denies nor cancels anything in the Biblical account. On the contrary, by creating a complete and living picture, it proves and substantiates the reality of heaven: it seems to say, "Look! here is the city of God, seen of old by St. John but seen today by a new traveller with a different pair of eyes and hence described differently."[6a] The very differences in the two pictures prove the truth of the new vision and the eternal reality of God's holy city. The picture given by the *Pearl* also corrects the fantastic picture of heaven presented by some fourteenth-century mystics.

A third idea of importance embodied in the *Pearl* has to do with the nature of beatitude. We have virtually lost the concept of eternal happiness in heaven and make fun of the idea of marching, playing a harp, and singing. But the Middle Ages had a different view: they knew that the singing and marching symbolized the beatific vision, the sight of God, and to see God meant to be one with him: to possess infinite power and love and knowledge and thus to live in one eternal orgasm that could never change or cloy or cease to delight. The *Pearl* shows this in its climactic scene and thereby also supports by divine revelation a concept denied by one of the Popes in the fourteenth century.

The debated point was whether or not the souls of the sainted dead possess the beatific vision – that is, whether they see God and thus become full participants in God's power and glory. Pope John XXII, in 1332, preached publicly that they do not – that the direct vision of God will not be theirs until the Last Day, when after the Resurrection their souls are reunited with their bodies.[7]

One can imagine the strong feelings this pronouncement would arouse: the indignation both of those who believed that their dead loved ones had been fully admitted into God's presence and also all those who relied for their own salvation upon the intercession of the sainted dead.

Nevertheless it was dangerous to contradict a Pope. Thomas Waleys, a Dominican educated at Oxford and Paris, found it so. On January 4, 1333, in the Pope's city of Avignon, in a speech before the Cardinals, he daringly challenged what John had said. Five days later he was charged with heresy and put in prison. A correspondence about his trial ensued between the King of France (Philip VI), the University of Paris, and Pope John; and eventually, after seventeen months of imprisonment, Waleys was released through the influence of the French court.[8]

The Pope, however, maintained the correctness of his view; but a formula was found to allow him to make this a personal view of his own but not a view binding upon the church.[9] On January 29, 1336, after the death of John, a new Pope, Benedict XII, pronounced judgment in favor of the saints' direct vision.[10] The *Pearl* not only shows the saved souls' direct vision of God, but its emotional climax comes with the ecstasy of that vision:

> Of sunne ne mone had þay no nede;
> þe self God watȝ her lompelyȝt,
> þe Lombe her lantyrne, ...   (1045-1047)

In the climactic scene (983-1152) still another idea of large import is dramatized. At the opening of the scene a procession forms in the heavenly city and moves toward the throne of God. This procession is made up of virgins wearing tall crowns of pearl and graceful, flowing surcoats of white, trimmed with an abundance of pearls (the virgins are apparently the same as those described in Revelation, but the details of dress are not mentioned there), and it is led by the Lamb of God. Immediately, in delight at the approach of the Lamb, the aldormen of heaven fall groveling to the ground and legions of angels are called together by what is happening. Then "glory and gle" are newly broached, and virgins and angels and all sing in love and adoration of the Lamb.

At this moment, when all attention centers upon the Lamb, who is best and happiest and "moste to pryse" of all things in heaven or earth, the narrator suddenly sees on his white side "a wounde ful wyde & weete" close to his heart (1135-1136). From that wound the blood spreads; but, though he is hurt, the Lamb shows no awareness of the pain or the wound. Instead, his looks are "gloryous glade" (1144) as the song of heaven strikes through the earth to hell.

This scene combines material from two scenes in Revelation (one in Chapter 14 describing the Lamb with the Virgins, and the other in Chapter 5 where the elders prostrate themselves, the angels gather, and every created thing in heaven, on earth, and under the earth praises the Lamb). In Revelation the Lamb is described "standing, as though it had been slain," and this has been interpreted to mean "Christ in his glorious manhood, having risen from the dead."[11] To what is said in Revelation the narrator of the *Pearl* adds the actual wound and the spreading blood and thus makes the scene a vision of Christ's eternal sacrifice for the salvation of mankind.[11a]

In this way the poem establishes by divine revelation the truth of a medieval belief in the heavenly sacrifice of Christ, a belief held by generations of medieval men, often expressed by medieval saints and thinkers, but not accepted as a dogma by the Church. To them the central event of history was the Incarnation and Sacrifice of Christ, and every other event from the Creation to the present moment either prefigured or reflected some happening connected with Christ's earthly life. It was therefore eminently proper that it should also occupy a central place in eternity, for Christ's sacrifice in heaven fulfilled and completed the medieval concept of world history. The idea entered actively into men's imagination and played a significant part in their concept of the Eucharist, as will be shown in Chapter VIII. To the author of *The Pearl* the scene of the Lamb's sacrifice in heaven doubtless represented a supreme moment – God revealing to man a mystery which had been only half-revealed before but was now made plain for all time to come through this new vision.

Probably the most pervading idea embodied in the *Pearl* is the basic concept on which the whole vast structure of medieval religion rested, the knowableness of God. To the dedicated believer the attaining of direct knowledge of God – through any possible means – was the goal of life. Full knowledge came only in heaven when one looked upon the face of God and became one with him; but on earth the knowledge one might attain was not only a foretaste of heaven but also the only means of reaching heaven. In St. Bernard's words,

> "...if you lack the knowledge of God, there is no hope for you."
> ...for you cannot love Him Whom you do not know, nor possess Him Whom you have not loved. Know thyself, therefore, that you may fear God; know Him, that you may love Him even as you fear...salvation is not possible without the fear and love of God. Other things do not matter one way or the other.[12]

The medieval Church accepted this view and built upon it, and the great minds of the Age of Faith elaborated and developed it. Saint Thomas Aquinas, for example, analyzed knowledge and blessedness and concluded that "the essence of beatitude is an act of mind."

Nevertheless, near the beginning of the fourteenth century, the concept came under powerful and destructive attack. Duns Scotus, employing all his resources of logic and dialectic, sought to show that God's ways are not understandable, that God himself cannot be known to man, and that man's blessedness must lie, therefore, not in knowledge, which he does not and cannot have, but "in the perfect functioning of his will in accordance with the will of God."[13] In Duns' thinking and reasoning is already implied the Protestant Reformation's emphasis on "conversion" – the subjection of one's will to Christ and the acceptance of Jesus as one's personal savior.

To Duns' attack William of Ockham added the razor sharpness of his thinking. Like Duns he held that "will and not intellect is the primary faculty of the soul,"[14] but he went beyond Duns in drawing a strict line between the material world, which man may examine intellectually, and the spiritual world, which is beyond man's comprehension. Thereby, intentionally or not, he established a premise for the denial of any ultimate reality beyond the material.

The *Pearl* makes answer to both Duns Scotus and Ockham. Dramatically it shows how knowledge of God came to one man. In a vision, through God's grace, the narrator stands in the revealing light of heaven and talks with one who, though a child, has looked into the face of God and therefore can say:

We þur3outly hauen cnawyng ...   (859)

The man is stubborn and stupid with the pride and blindness of earthly creatures, but the being from heaven refuses to abandon him and ever so patiently and wisely goes over his lesson in new and revealing ways till he cannot help beginning to see.[14a]   Finally, through favor utterly undeserved, he is directed to a hill from which he is permitted to look into the New Jerusalem and see God and thus receives one moment of piercing illumination that alters him forever.

In this way The *Pearl* demonstrates that God is knowable[14b] and infinitely lovable and gracious beyond any conceivable merit of man himself. It does not deny the importance of subjecting one's will to God – "Lorde, mad hit arn þat agayn þe stryuen," the narrator says in next-to-the-last stanza – but it places its continuing emphasis on knowledge – self-knowledge and knowledge of God.

This does not exhaust the religious content of the *Pearl*, but is enough to show that the poem is a serious, thoughtful, and imaginative presentation of the faith that gave the Middle Ages their special character.

Chapter II

Endnotes

1. *Dante's Convivio*, tr. William Walrond Jackson (London: Oxford University Press, 1909), pp. 131, 20.

2. Preface to *De Causa Dei contra Pelagium*, ed. 1618, cited by Carleton Brown, PMLA 19 (1904), 129-130.

3. *Le Opere di Dante Alighiere*, a cura del Edward Moore, rivedute nel testo dal Paget Toynbee (quarta edizione) (Oxford, 1924), p. 107.

3a. Jill Mann argues that the *Pearl* sets up a complex opposition between human desire signified by the iterated word "more" and heavenly plenitude signified by the iterated term "innoghe." The heavenly economy is a profoundly paradoxical one where "renunciation is rewarded with satisfaction. In its fullness the desire for 'more' falls away, not because one prudently settles for 'less' but because that endless desire is endlessly satisfied, and it is the completeness of that satisfaction that constitutes 'enough'" (30). She points out that "the use of the word 'paye' in the sense of 'satisfaction' at the beginning and end of the poem inevitably colors the use of the word 'payed' in the maiden's statement that everyone is 'payed inlyche' in the kingdom of heaven and makes it into a kind of pun: all are equally 'paid' because all are equally 'satisfied' – that is everyone has *enough*" (25).

Glending Olson points to a similar paradox when he discusses the inability of the human opposition – "reste" verses "travayle" – to accomodate the vitally active *quies* of Heaven (425).

Milroy interprets the parable in the same way as Mann: "There is no question of more or less in God's kingdom....He gives freely and generously to those who are chosen, and this generosity is simply 'enough' – not 'more,' not 'less' (202).

Johnson argues that by concentrating on the equity of the parable, "we run the risk..., like the narrator" of losing "the parable's message. The maiden uses the parable to illustrate the necessity for spiritual labor because man must work in order to deserve the 'peny' which is like the kingdom of heaven" (186).

4. *Cap. Maiores, Decret.* 1, 3 tit. 42 de baptismo, quoted by Pohle, *Lehrbuch der Dogmatik*, II, 554, and cited by Wellek, *loc. cit.*, p. 21, note 88.

5. Clement, de summa Trinit. et fide cath., also quoted by Pohle and cited by Wellek, pp. 21-22, note 89.

6. *The Poetical Works of Chaucer*, ed. F. N. Robinson (Boston: Houghton Mifflin, 1933), p. 567.

6a. Rosalind Field points out that 'while the approach to the city shows the poet departing from his source material in the Apocalypse, the account of the sight that meets the Dreamer's gaze from the hilltop vantage point in section 17 is...closely dependent on that source" (8). She sees several formal reasons for this paraphrase-like section: "First, in the pacing of the poem, it acts as a delaying device between the dramatic interchange of dialogue and the drama of the culminating vision...The second purpose of section 17, with its concatenation phrase 'þe Apostle John,' is to establish the objective authority of the vision...Having thus established the authenticity of the Dreamer's vision, the poet is free in the next section to select and emphasize the details with which to develop his main themes" (8-9). The poet "infuse[s] the vision of Heaven" "in section 19" "with a 'delyt' it does not have in the awesome majesty of the original" (10).

Like Rosalind Field, Larry Sklute argues that the paraphrase of John provides an authoritative counterweight to the limited perceptions of a naive narrator (676). Similarly, Bogdanos states that "the poet rather daringly appropriates the anagogic telos of the Bible 'because' he wants his poem read as an analogue of God's word" (11).

By contrast, Ann Watts sees John being set up as an antithetical figure to the narrator: "John of Patmos saw the New Jerusalem and uttered no inexpressibility: yet *Pearl* lifting much from this source contains inexpressibilities" (32). In other words, John's eloquence serves to accentuate the narrator's inadequacy.

Sandra Prior argues, in her dissertation, that *Pearl* reflects "a tension" "between the private lyric experience and the apocalyptic mode"; this tension is mediated by the Eucharist (974-975A).

7.   G. Mollat, *The Popes at Avignon*, tr. Janet Love (Edinburgh: Thomas Nelson and Sons, 1949), pp. 21-22.

8.   "Wallensis or Waleys, Thomas," DNB, lix, 121-122.

9.   Mollat, *op. cit.*, p. 23.

10.   *Ibid.*, p. 28.

11.   Darwell Stone, *A History of the Doctrine of the Holy Eucharist*, (London: Longmans Green, 1909), I, 17.

11a. Rosalind Field points out how original this representation of the Lamb is: while iconographic manuscripts of the period sometimes represent the wounded lamb in earlier chapters of Revelation, there is a "consistent absence of wounds where the Lamb appears in triumph" (13). She points out that "as a reminder of human suffering, the flaw in the perfection of the Lamb's pearl-like fleece is directly relevant to the main problem examined by the poem which opens with a bereaved narrator who cannot accept death....The final part of his vision is of an eternal city in which suffering and death are transmuted into joy" (15).
      Prior argues in her dissertation that the Eucharist "which unites personal with universal and eternal with historical in a sacramental event mediates the tension between private lyric experience and the

apocalyptic mode" (974-975A). Similarly, Larry Sklute states that while "the perpetual communion, the bliss of heaven "is" not available to the living man," "the Eucharist" offers him "the bliss of heaven here on earth" (679).

Bogdanos rather fancifully argues that the figure of the bleeding lamb creates "an alienating grotesqueness" which reflects "the disturbing transference between ravishment and self-devastation, between ecstacy and death, suggesting an indefinite kinship between them in the anagogic experience" (139). To see the image of the bleeding lamb as an alienating grotesque figure is to impose a twentieth-century category on a medieval Christian poem.

12. *Santi Bernardi Opera*, ed. J. Leclercq et al. (Rome: Editiones Cistercienses, 1958), II, Sermo xxxvii, I, i, p. 9. The translation is by a religious of C. S. M. V., *Saint Bernard on the Song of Songs* (London: A. R. Mowbray & Co.; New York: Morehouse-Gorham, 1952), p. 110.

13. Henry Osborn Taylor, *The Medieval Mind* (London: Macmillan, 1911: 2nd ed., 1914), II, 471.

14. *Encyclopaedia Britannica* (University of Chicago, 1948), XVI, 679.

14a. Ann Schotter approaches this issue from a slightly different, specifically linguistic angle. How does one translate an apprehension of the divine into fallen human language? She points out that "one solution is to suggest it by various analogical devices while at the same time using a naïve dreamer as a warning against taking literally." Another device, she suggests, is to promiscuously mingle "the most splendid resources of the medium" with "some of its pedestrian" *topoi* "as a warning against excessive trust in language" (23). The narrator might apprehend the divine, but the reader can only "know" his vision through language whose mediatory nature the poet unobtrusively emphasizes through his use of stock rhetorical devices.

Ann Chalmers Watts points out that the narrator's use of the "inexpressibility topos" is very different from the orthodox Christian view of ineffability. Language fails the narrator because of his all-too-human desire: "*Pearl*'s two brief inexpressibilities, at the beginning and ending of the dream, link failed language to heavenly vision broken by desire. The two longer inexpressibilities...make more explicit *Pearl's* unusual connection between words that cannot say and failed flesh that in its weakness, still desires" (32).

Lynn Johnson emphasizes the gap between the maiden's comprehension of language and the narrator's linguistic ineptness—"The lessons the maiden will teach the narrator are the lessons of ...language" (166). The dreamer's "use of language" "is literal and limited," "rigid and legalistic"; "the maiden, "by contrast," frequently uses words in their metaphoric sense" (167). Wilson makes a similar point: "What the girl does is to take the narrator's imagery and give it different referends, supernal for earthly. Thus it is an index of the narrator's progress in understanding when we see him using the same linguistic habits as a girl" (124).

14b.   However, Stephen Russell stresses that the narrator's "knowledge" is achieved through contemplation rather than ratiocination. He argues that the poem valorizes "mystical" "contemplation" over "eschatalogical meditation" (190) and that "the error of the narrator...is the error of eschatology in general, the error in seeking to comprehend the eternal and supernal joy of Salvation in rational, logical terms" (189).

CHAPTER III

WROUGHT EXQUISITELY UNDER A VEIL

A distinctive theory of poetry was created in the Middle Ages. Rooted in Biblical interpretation and medieval theology, it held that the subject matter of poetry should be presented "under a veil" and "should necessarily be clothed in metrical or rhythmical beauty and adorned with all the colours of rhetoric" so that, as Roger Bacon said, "the beauty and musical qualities of the writing will entice the reader to love of virtue and hatred of evil, just as passages in the Bible entice the reader to divine wisdom and bring men near to the mysteries of God."[1]

In accordance with this theory the poet was advised "not to speak plainly, but to talk in such terms as only the initiated could understand." This, as St. Jerome had said, would keep a a writer's "truths from becoming cheap and vulgar; it would also render his truths more precious, seeing that they were won only after effort."[2] Moreover, such a manner of speaking was consonant with God's own way, for every object and happening in the world is a revelation of God's mind, but the meaning becomes apparent only to those who are able to look through and beyond the factual to the eternal.

In pursuance of these goals, medieval poetry used every kind of symbolism and figurative language for the ostensible purpose of challenging the reader's attention and forcing him to use his own mind to interpret what was being indirectly or figuratively said. It also stressed lavish imagery, beauty of sound, and elaborate workmanship. Intricate rhyme-schemes were invented, and various devices were developed for linking lines, stanzas, cantos, or other divisions, and the beginnings and endings of poems. In addition a startling variety of patterns were employed for balancing, contrasting, and repeating words, or different forms of the same word, or different words containing the same stem, or phrases or refrains, in such a way as to provide emphasis on an idea, or on the varied meanings of a single word or phrase, or to create a haunting or ironic or surprising effect.

This kind of poetry, with its emphasis on veiling and embellishment, was lifted to the level of art in the late thirteenth and early fourteenth centuries by Dante and the writers of what he called the *dolce stil nuovo* (the sweet new style), who not only fused the language and ideas of courtly, chivalric love with religious and philosophical thinking and feeling but also set new standards of style and form in accord with "a clearer consciousness of art."[3] Their aim, apparently, was to control and unify all the manifold elements of composition in such a way as to make their subtle and complex verse seem inviting, urgent, beautiful, and alive.

Such poetry was held in great esteem in its day. Boccaccio, for example, gave it the highest possible praise. "Whatever is composed under a veil and thus exquisitely wrought," he said, "that, and that only, is poetry."[4]

The *Pearl* exemplifies the medieval theory and method. It is subtle and indirect, challenging the reader's attention both by what it says and what it withholds. The characters are portrayed dramatically, without explanatory comment – the child by appearance, dress, manners, gestures, expression, tone of speech, response to the man, and by numberless little touches that make her seem alive and individual; the man mainly by what he sees, thinks, feels, and says, but also by what the child sees in him and makes evident by her responses to him. There is a paradoxical combination of frankness and reticence: the reader feels he has been taken into the narrator's confidence and is about to learn his inmost secrets; but he is never told directly the man's name, or status, or the child's name, or even the man's relationship to the child.

Likewise the scene is presented without explanation. Vivid details are introduced as they bear on the moment's events and the altering consciousness of the narrator; but the place is never identified and the reader is not even told what it is – a cemetery, or the herb-garden of a monastery, or an orchard, or something more.

In the same way the action proceeds without directly answering any of the reader's questions. The poem begins with a dramatic scene and moves on breathlessly to one dramatic scene after another. It strictly avoids any exposition of antecedent action and touches on past situations only briefly and ambiguously through what the characters say and what the narrator thinks or remembers at moments when the past impinges on the present.[4a]

Fashioned under this veiling, the *Pearl* exhibits the richness of imagery, beauty of sound, and elaborateness of workmanship characteristic of this kind of poetry.[4b] It also shows an almost incredible combination of devices for linking parts and stressing words and ideas. Twelve-lines stanzas with interlocking rhyme (ababababbcbc) are linked together in groups of five by a "key-word" which appears as the last word of the last line in each stanza. The same key-word or word-stem also appears in the first line of stanzas 2, 3, 4, 5, and 6, thus linking the first group with the next. All 101 stanzas in the poem are thus linked except for a break between stanzas 60 and 61. That break cuts the poem into two main parts, and is bridged by the linking of stanza 61 with stanza 1 through repetition of meaning, "wythouten spotte" in stanza 1 being replaced by "maskelle$_3$," both signifying stainless. The beginning and the ending of the poem are also linked, "Perle plesaunte to prynces paye" (line 1) furnishing key-words repeated nine times in the last five stanzas, including the final line.

Morris, ten Brink, and Gollancz, creators of the orthodox interpretation, viewed the *Pearl* as a simple expression of grief by a primitive poet; but later scholars have seen it very differently.

Osgood (1906) was the first to call attention to the complexity of emotion in the poem. The narrator's feelings, he wrote, at first "seem multifarious and almost spasmodic; they appear successively as poignant grief, despondency, resentment, love, joy, quick reaction to grief and impatience; then indignation and humility in confused succession, resolving by degrees into ecstatic transport, which subsides into quiet regret, and lastly into perfect tranquility. But, multifarious as they may seem, [these feelings] are but various manifestations of...a subtle and urgent yearning for peace," and it is by the unity of this underlying emotion that "the widely discrepant elements of the poem...are combined and wrought into one artistic whole."[5]

It was Osgood also who first directed attention to the blending of courtly, chivalric love with religious feeling. After commenting on the large and subtle influence of chivalry that pervades the *Pearl*, he pointed out that the narrators' lament (11-24, 241-252, *passim*) and his description of the "lady" (162-240, *passim*) both employ the style of the poets of chivalry. "Furthermore, the language and ecstasy of chivalric love are transferred to unworldly objects, as in the representation of Christ receiving his bride (413-420), and in the adoration of the Virgin (425-444). Indeed a certain ecstatic quality prevails in the poems, which, though characteristic of the age of chivalry, is broader and deeper than the formal boundaries of that institution."[6]

Ten Brink and Gollancz saw no structural unity in the *Pearl*, but later scholars found it to be an artistic whole, complex in nature, intricately put together, with all its parts integrated so as to move forward to a central climax and denouement. The conflict, in Charles Moorman's analysis (1955), is between diametrically opposed points of view – the earthly and the divine – and each part of the mid-section is an essential step in the narrator's movement from rebellion and ignorance to understanding and acceptance. The long debate between the narrator and the child from heaven, Moorman believes, constitutes the only means by which the struggle could be brought to a resolution.

> For it becomes quite clear in the course of the conversation...that their differences are profound. He is a man, she an angel...Earth cannot receive her; he is not ready for heaven. The debate in which they engage thus becomes a contest...between a point of view which sees natural death only as an irreducible paradox of decay and growth and a point of view which can reconcile that paradox in terms of a higher unity.[7]

The Victorians also minimized the figurative side of the *Pearl*; modern scholars, on the other hand, have emphasized it. Readers, Conley warned (1955), must be prepared to cope not only with "subtlety of definition" but also with "subtlety of aspect, especially in the form of irony, of work-play, and of metaphor." The poem, he concluded, is "deeply ironic."[8]

Though the Victorians, with the exception of Morris, recognized "the wealth and brilliancy of the poet's description,"[9] they and their followers tended to find serious fault with his diction. They thought the poet was not master of his medium and sometimes used the wrong word or "manufactured" a word in order to maintain the alliteration or provide a needed rhyme. They also believed he distorted syntax and meaning in order to repeat various words in accordance with the pattern of stanza-linking used in the poem.

More recent interpreters, on the contrary, have found everywhere in the *Pearl* the evidence of artistry with words.[9a] For instance, Wendell S. Johnson, in his analysis of the poem's diction and imagery (1953),[10] pointed out that the different meanings of each of the key-words, used ten times in positions required by the stanzaic form and the system of linking, are played against each other with subtlety and sureness so as to convey contrasts, mark points of emphasis, and suggest, at one and the same time, both complexity and an underlying identity, such words being used with "conscious ambiguity."

Johnson and others have also called attention to the poet's use of individual words and images for suggestion and implication, and the power and economy resulting from such use. For instance, the word *syngulere* in the first stanza of the poem, Fletcher (1921) pointed out, would have immediately caught the attention of any fourteenth-century reader and suggested the Virgin Mary because of the variations rung upon it by medieval religious writers in their praises of the Mother of God. Likewise the poet's comparison of the maiden's color to that of pearl would have suggested not only that the maiden's complexion was "not pallid, but warm with rose color," but also that she was to be linked with the Virgin, for red and white were colors symbolically connected with the Virgin.[11]

Hoffman, calling attention to the use of *flor-de-lys* and *rose* as symbols for the maiden, cites the poet's creation of a flower, garden, jewel, maiden identification related to the death-and-resurrection motif in the poem.

The jewel symbol suggests permanence and stability; the flower image is a reminder of mortality and the cycle of life.[12]

In the main part of his study[13] Johnson was primarily concerned with the poet's artistry in creating a complex pattern of imagery that contributes both to the poem's central meaning and its unity of effect. The poem's images, Johnson showed, "can in the main be divided into two groups; on the one hand, images out of the world of growing things, images of the garden and the vineyard which are associated with the dust of the earth; on the other, images of light and brilliant, light-reflecting gems, free of any spot (dust) and associated with whiteness and emblems of royalty."

These two sets of images begin in the very first lines of the poem: the pearl is "small, round, smooth, and *reken*, noble or radiant" (the one word implies both nobility and radiance), but it is lost in the *erbere* (garden or orchard), where the brightly colored flowers shine in the sun and cast their shadows on the dark mold. From the beginning, he also shows, the nine-times-repeated key-word in each stanza-group is chosen to contribute to the image pattern.

> The key word in the second stanza-group is *dubbement*, splendor, with the participial form meaning *arrayed*, and the imagery presents transfigured phenomena, the world arrayed in a strange glory: all is shining, shimmering, gleaming, glowing, flaming, bright; the colors have an incredible brilliance; and the very gravel on the ground is pearl. The effect which the poet describes is that of supremely intense light cast upon all natural objects, the basic image being one of *reflected* brilliance.

The image structure in the following sections, Johnson continues, "represents a progression toward the fuller understanding of this symbolic picture: the contrasting impressions of earth and of another place associated with jewelry, brightness, royalty." The ninth section presents a new aspect of the contrast: here "bodily labor is opposed to royal reward, and earthly time to divine timelessness."

> Date [the key word in this section] is used in the senses of *position, limit* ('þer is no date of hys goodness' - 493), *season, goal, time.* In God's mercy there is no limit, time, or season (the rich ambiguity of the word here is exploited by the whole passage],...

Throughout the poem the contrast between the earthly and the eternal is carried forward, amplified, and intensified[13a] through images that serve to extend and enlarge the reader's vision from the "erbere" at the beginning to a view that includes both heaven and earth – the world with its gardens and vineyards "where fertility is purchased only by toil and by death," and the New Jerusalem "with its perfect hardness and constancy, its brilliance and purity."

By means of a third set of symbols – introduced at the middle of the poem and carried forward from there – the poem presents the link between heaven and earth: the blood and water from Christ's side, symbolized by the water of baptism and the wine of the Eucharist.

Because they assumed the *Pearl* to be naive self-expression the Victorians never gave the slightest attention to the author's use of point of view. Later scholars, however, have studied it carefully and with admiration. Moorman, in his study of the role of the narrator (1955),[14] shows that the *Pearl* is developed from "a clearly defined and wholly consistent point of view," with everything that happens being seen and felt only as it strikes the attention of one person, the "I" of the poem.

> In terms of Henry James, the narrator-poet is the 'central intelligence' of the poem, in those of Brooks and Warren, the poem is the narrator's story, in that we are never allowed to see and judge the experience presented by the poem objectively and for ourselves but are, instead, forced, by the point of view which the poet adopts, to accept the experience of the vision only in terms of its relationship to him. The mind of the narrator in *Pearl*, like the mind of Strether in *The Ambassadors* or, to come closer home, the mind of Dante, the voyager, is the real subject under consideration. It is with the figure of the narrator alone in an "erbere" that the poem begins and ends;...

Not only is every sensation filtered through the consciousness of the narrator, but he himself is changed by what happens, and, in order for the reader to see and understand, these changes are foreshadowed, so that the very beginning of the poem implies the things that are to follow, even to the end. Thus a complex relationship is set up between the "I" as author, who "knows the whole story in advance," and the "I" as character in the story, who "meets everything freshly for the first time."[14a]

The two perspectives together produce a sort of stereoptical effect, that of an objective and partially mysterious reality. Furthermore, the poem presents some of the most difficult mysteries of religion, and these also are presented through the mind of the narrator, who does not understand them at all, to begin with, and wins, even at the end, to only a partial understanding. In this regard the narrator is presented in such a way as to fill the role of an Old Testament prophet – one who becomes spokesman for truths he himself does not understand.

In all these respects the handling of point of view is like that of Dante in the *Commedia*, for he also filters every sensation through the mind of the narrator and likewise provides a double perspective through "I" as author and "I" as character and, furthermore, reveals religious truths beyond the narrator's understanding. We may think of the narrator as merely Dante himself; but Dante, conscious of the technical aspects of viewpoint, spoke of the narrator as the *agent*, the individual who acts and is acted upon.[15] Both he and the author of the *Pearl* used the point of view of the *agent* with full understanding of its requirements and its purpose. Both did so with great skill.

In another respect (not entirely intelligible to us, but characteristically medieval) the *Commedia* and the *Pearl* show similarity: in both number is employed as an "architectural element." Dante used 1 (Unity), 3 (Trinity), and 100 (a perfect number) in the construction of the *Commedia*: 3 lines in each stanza, 1 introductory canto, 33 cantos about the descent into Hell, 33 cantos each in the *Purgatory* and the *Paradise*, 100 cantos in all.[16] Similarly the author of the *Pearl* used 12 and its multiples (related to Plato's number governing the universe and the life of man[17]) in shaping his poem: 12 lines in each stanza, 60 lines in each group of stanzas, 12 groups in Part I and 1212 lines in the whole.

In spite of similarities (including the obvious ones in subject matter) it may be a mistake to assume that the author of the *Pearl* knew Dante's work[17a]: rather, being thoroughly familiar with veiled poetry and the technical advances associated with the fourteenth-century flowering of religious poetry, he may simply have written in that tradition, in his own way and style, without any direct Dantean influence.

Chapter III

Endnotes

1.　Op. Tertium (R. S.), lxiv, 266, quoted by J. W. H. Atkins, *English Literary*.

2.　Ep., liii, cited by Atkins, p. 20.

3.　Francisco de Sanctis, *History of Italian Literature*, tr. Joan Redfern (New York: Harcourt Brace, 1931), I, 51, 55-59.

4.　Giovanni Boccaccio, *Genealogie Deorum Gentilium Libri* (Bari: Gius, Laterza & Figli, 1951), II, xiv, 7, ad fin. The Latin text reads as follows: *Mera poesis est quicquid sub velamento componitur et exponitur exquisite*. Cf. Translation by Charles G. Osgood, Jr., *Boccaccio on Poetry* (New York: Liberal Arts Press, 1956), p. 42.

4a.　Sklute agrues that the ambiguities in the poem act educatively for the reader. We are made to experience vicariously the naive narrator's attempt to comprehend divine paradox, and in the process, we are educated (664).

　　　　Davenport, like Sklute, declares that "our understanding of the poem depends on our understanding of the process through which the first person narrator is going" (34).

4b.　Cary Nelson in an elegant essay argues that the "intricately articulated language and detailed linkage between stanzas" creates a "circular structure" that "is integral to our most vital experience of the poem and its vision....Form and content in *Pearl* are not simply parallel or complementary – they are the same" (27).

5.　*The Pearl*, ed. Osgood, p. lxii.

6.　*Ibid*., p. xlii.

　　　　Davenport in a more recent reading makes a similar claim – "the opening stanzas" have "an intensity which is closer to the manner of courtly love lyric than that usual in a vision poem. At first, the narrator speaks of his loss in disguise, like the anguished lover protecting the name of his soverign lady..." (8).

　　　　Wilson too points out that "much of the language which the narrator uses to express his sense of loss and desolation is congruous...with the anguish which a man might feel at the death of a loved lady" (118).

　　　　Lynn Johnson links the transforming dialogue between the narrator and the Pearl maiden to an epithalmiun, and she points out how "the epithalmium" was "frequently linked with the figure of Magdalene and in particular with the literal and figurative understanding of her encounter with Christ in John 20" (207).

7.　Charles Moorman, "The Role of the Narrator in *Pearl*, MP 53 (1955), p. 77, second column.

8.   John Allen Conley, *Pearl* and a Lost Tradition, JEGP 54 (1955), 339.

9.   *Pearl*, ed. Gollancz (1921), p. xxvi.

9a.   Jill Mann argues that the poet's artful repetition of link words like "more" and "innoghe" establishes a thematic opposition between unsatiated human desire and a heavenly plenitude that is paradoxically achieved through renunciation (Mann, 30). She also demonstrates the way in which the poet plays with the two senses of the word "paye" to underline the gap between a heavenly and human economy (25).
      Davenport discusses some parts of the dialogue, where the refrain words apply differently to the Dreamer and to the Maiden, or where new meanings seem to grow out of old ones. At times the two points of view meet and separate through the prism of the repeated phrase and the play of shifting senses creates effects of dramatic antithesis and irony" (43).
      Wilson discusses the way in which the dialogic reverberation of certain key terms (like "dele") dialectically transforms them – that is, in the process of the same term being exchanged between narrator and Maiden, certain key terms are transformed and gain a powerful thematic resonance (cf. bibliography for citation).
      Bogdanos discusses the "startling economy and ingenuity" with which the Pearl poet transforms the linking refrain. He argues that "the word-play incarnates in verbal form the process of development of the poem's central imagery" (55).

10.   Wendell Stacy Johnson, "The Imagery and Diction of *The Pearl*: Toward an Interpretation," ELH 20 (1953), 161-180.

11.   *Ibid.*, 165-179. Quotations from 165, 166, 168, 172, 178-179.

12.   Stanton Hoffman, "*The Pearl*, Notes for an Interpretation," MP, 58 (November, 1960), p. 79.

13.   Wendell Stacy Johnson, "The Imagery and Diction of *The Pearl*: Toward an Interpretation," ELH 20 (1953), 161-180.

13a. Bogdanos discusses the complex role that flower imagery plays in the poem: "The beauty of the flowers...evokes a dual response. It blunts grief and assuages the ugliness of death – only to exacerbate it the next moment, intensifying the ugliness by standing in poignant contrast to it....The 'huyle' becomes a sumptuously ornamented grave mound; the heavy fragrance of its spices and the damp overripeness around it exude a powerful odor of mortality. Opulence turns into decay" (28).

14.   Moorman, *loc. cit.*, 74, first column.

14a. Bogdanos strongly argues for a distinction between narrator and poet; he sees this distinction as crucial to our proper reading experience of the poem's irony (33).

James Milroy discusses the connection between language and point of view in a provocative essay. He argues that the "sober formal address" of the Maiden contrasts strongly "with the passionate," often wrong-headed "tone of the dreamer" (198). Both maiden and dreamer are carefully constructed products of a poet.

Davenport, less convincingly, argues that there are three figures in the poem – poet and a double voiced narrator –." The Dreamer ostensibly a consistent voice throughout the poem really has two different voices. One voice speaks movingly of pain and loss....[The other is a] stooge who feeds the Sunday school teacher with leading questions" (25). Davenport's derisive terms betray a rather insensitive modern reader wilfully refusing to give the medieval Christian text its *donée*.

Carroll in chapters 1 and 2 of his dissertation discusses "the new traditional separation between poet and narrator, and re-examines that division in relation to the special circumstances in and for which medieval poetry was composed – especially the practice of oral delivery and presentation to specific local audience" (2336A).

Larry Sklute sets up a third term to be taken into account: the reader. He argues that "Pearl seeks to demonstrate how we readers learn what we learn by describing the frustrations that occur between our expectations for the dreamer and our failure with him to comprehend rationally...our struggle to understand – and not our understanding – accounts for our satisfaction upon completion of the poem" (664). Sklute's reading (very reminiscent of Stanley Fish's reading of *Paradise Lost* in *Surprised by Sin*) sets up a gap between narrator and reader brought about by the poetic voice as expressed through the tutelary pearl maiden. We identify with the narrator; hence, the errors he makes educate us vicariously.

Davenport, like Sklute, declares that "our understanding of the poem depends on our understanding of the process through which the first person narrator is going" (34). Unlike Sklute, however, Davenport is skeptical about the poem's unity: he envisions the reader confronted by a tension between asserted doctrine and realized feeling (53).

Bogdanos argues "that the reader is placed by the poet at a superior level of evaluation....The discrepancy in the perception of symbolic realities between the narrator and the reader...creates in the reader anxiety and dramatic suspense."

James Paul makes a similar argument in his dissertation: "*Pearl* comes to an *aporia*, a point at which the narrator fails, in order that the reader may succeed in resolving the dialectic of the poem" (3476A).

Hendrix, using Fish's categories of "self-satisfying works [that] affirm rational and discursive structures" versus "self-comsuming works" that "subvert" them (459), argues that *Pearl* by subverting the reader's expectations and by confounding rational logic forces him or her to see the essentially mysterious nature of divine 'purpose.'

15. Francis Fergusson, *Dante's Drama of the Mind: A Modern Reading of the Purgatorio* (Princeton University Press, 1953), p. 10. The quoted

words are part of Fergusson's description of Dante's use of point of view, but they apply equally well to the *Pearl* poet's.

16   Epistola X (letter to Can Grande), *le Opere di Dante Alighiere*, p. 417, paragraph 14. Cf. Charles Sterrett Latham, *A Translation of Dante's Eleven Letters*, ed. George Rice Carpenter (Boston: Houghton Mifflin, 1892), pp. 198-199; also the definitions of *agere* in *A New Latin Dictionary* (Harper's Latin Dictionary) ed. E. A. Andrews, revised by Charles T. Lewis and Charles Short (New York: American Book Company, 1879; rptd. 1907), pp. 74-75.

17.   *The Republic of Plato*, ed., Francis MacDonald Cornford (New York, London: Oxford University Press, 1968), viii, section 546, p. 265. There have been several studies that have examined numerological play in the *Pearl* poem. Coolidge Chapman compares the use of numerological patterning in the *Divine Commedia* and *Pearl*; Maren-Sofie Rostvig discusses the symbolic appropriateness of the significant numbers − 5, 6, 8, 12, 60, and 101; and Barbara Nolan considers the symbolism of numbers in the *Pearl* poem.

17a.   P. M. Kean, on the contrary, argues that it is very likely that the Pearl poet had read Dante (Kean's argument paraphrased in Schotter, 28).

CHAPTER IV

DANTE'S GUIDE TO VEILED POETRY

To read veiled poetry with understanding, a modern reader needs some knowledge of medieval multi-level interpretation of literature. A definite system was first formulated in the third century by Origen, who described three levels of meaning in the Bible: the literal, the moral, and the spiritual. In the next century Hilary of Poitiers devised another level, called the allegorical. According to this type of interpretation, everything in the Bible was to be taken as a reflection or a prefigurement of Christ's incarnation. Hilary says:

> Every word contained in the sacred volume announces by word, explains by facts, and corroborates by examples the coming of our Lord Jesus,...In each personage, in every age, and in every act, the image of his coming, of his teaching, of his resurrection, and of our Church, is reflected as in a mirror.[1]

These four levels, then, were combined to create the fourfold system of allegorical interpretation, which first appeared in complete form in the works of John Cassian in the fifth century, became common property in the ninth century, and was in general use from the ninth to the middle of the fourteenth.[2]

At this point a closer look at the words *allegorical* and *allegory* should be in order, for they have been at the base of many a fruitless argument about the *Pearl*. Indeed there was a time when it seemed that three scholars could talk about allegory in the *Pearl* and each mean a different thing and each misunderstand the other.

In the system described above allegory means two things, and two only: (1) on all four levels, "the veiled presentation...of a meaning metaphorically implied, but not expressly stated";[3] (2) on level 2, a reflection or prefigurement of Christ's incarnation. It does *not* mean what most modern readers would take it to mean: personification, i.e., the representation of ideas as persons.[4]

The medieval system, employed constantly in sermons, was rooted in the belief that the material world is a finite expression of the infinite mind of God; and it followed the reasoning that although God expresses himself in every object and happening in the universe, his full meaning cannot be seen in any isolated object or happening, but is to be found, instead, in the interrelationships of things and events, which, when properly understood, both constitute and reveal "the pattern of the universe."

Accordingly medieval symbolism was linked with the medieval theory of the four sources of knowledge – nature, scripture, reason, and revelation – and the four levels of allegorical interpretation were joined in the proper order with the four sources; the literal meaning level 1, with nature, i.e., the material world or the world of fact; the allegorical, level 2, with the Bible, the record of Christ's incarnation; the moral, or tropological, level 3, with Christian morality, regarded as the natural and proper field for the exercise of man's reason; and the anagogical, or spiritual, level 4, with the eternal, which can be known only through revelation.

Over the centuries this system of interpretation came to be applied not only to the Bible but to other sacred documents such as saints' lives, then to the Roman classics, and finally to all kinds of writings. The result was inevitable: the system was made ridiculous by crude misapplications. For instance, in *Gesta Romanorun*, at the end of the story of Androcles and the lion, the compiler tells the reader that the lion "is crist [Christ], that halteth in the foot, that is, in man that is his membre, for he is hede [head], and we are his membres. Speaking of such "moralisations," Warton in his history of English literature (1781) made the following comments:

> This was an age of vision and mystery; and every work was believed to contain a double, or secondary meaning. Nothing escaped this eccentric spirit of refinement and abstraction; and, together with the Bible, as we have seen, not only the general

history of ancient times was explained allegorically, but even
the poetical fictions of the classics were made to signify the
great truths of religion, with a degree of boldness, and a want
of discrimination, which in another age would have acquired
the character of the most profane levity, if not of absolute
impiety.[5]

In Dante's time a revision and purification of the system was underway. As Dante explained in the *Convivio*,[6] poets who followed the system were inclined to substitute a different meaning for that which the churchmen expected on level 2; i.e., they discarded the idea of everything mirroring Christ's incarnation and offered, instead, an implied idea or theme, a hidden truth. He also made plain that the literal meaning is the basis and source of all the other meanings, and that it would be impossible and irrational to give attention to the other meanings, especially the second level, without first understanding the literal. He further pointed out that whenever a fourth level is included, the literal account gives intimation of supernal things.

Apparently Dante did not believe that every veiled work contained all four levels of meaning, and was wary about trying to express hidden meanings in a few sententious words as the churchmen did. In discussing his own work both in the *Convivio* and in the *Vita Nuova* he spent most of his space showing how to understand the literal meaning.

Here is his description of the system:

...books can be understood, and ought to be explained, in four principal senses. One is called literal, and this it is which goes no farther than the letter, such as the simple narration of the thing you treat.
The second is the allegorical, and this is the meaning hidden under the cloak of fables, and is a truth concealed beneath a fair fiction; as when Ovid says that Orpheus with his lute tamed wild beasts and moved trees and rocks; which means that the wise man, with the instrument of his voice, softens and humbles cruel hearts, and moves at his will those who live neither for science nor for art, and those, who, having no rational life whatever, are almost like stones....
The third sense is called moral; and this readers should carefully gather from all writings, for the benefit of themselves and their descendants; it is such as we may gather from the Gospel, when Christ went up into the mountain to be transfigured, and of the twelve disciples took with him but

three; which in the moral sense may be understood thus, that in
most secret things we should have few companions.

The fourth is called anagogical, that is, above the
senses.[7]

The four-level system, even as described by Dante, may seem strange
and repulsive to modern readers, but it has more relevance to us than one
might think. As a matter of fact every great story is raised in some manner
from the specific to the universal, and this is usually done by a pattern of
symbols even though the reader may not be conscious of the fact. In this
sense the medieval system, as specified by Dante, is a statement of the basic
truths of symbolism used by all writers in all ages and has been so recognized
by some modern critics. For example, Caroline Gordian and Allen Date cite
the above passage from Dante as "a practical explanation of the ways in
which various symbols fuse to convey the author's meaning." They go on to
say:

> The anagogical level is not ordinarily the concern of fiction
> writers, who write of events that take place in this world, not
> the next. But in any masterpiece of fiction – even masterpieces
> of realism – the action operates on the three other levels.

They then illustrate the three levels of meaning by analysis of Ernest
Hemingway's "The Killers." On the literal level, they say, this is

> ...a story of what happened one evening to Nick Adams, an
> adolescent boy who used to hang around a diner. Nick's horror
> at the knowledge that Ole Andreson is going to be murdered
> embodies his moral conviction that it is wrong for one man to
> kill another. Allegorically, the story sets forth a boy's dawning
> realization that every man lives, for the most part, alone, and
> dies alone.[8]

The *Pearl*, though written after the middle of the fourteenth century,
follows the system described above. It makes use of veiling, as shown in
Chapter III. It used many-faceted symbols: for example, the word *perle* is
used to mean the child that was lost, the gem, the name of the child, the soul,
eternal life, the goal of man's life on earth, and the state of blessedness in
heaven.[8a] Furthermore, the poem itself demonstrates and attests the
author's familiarity with the fourfold system by including several allegorical
interpretations of passages from the Bible:

1. In lines 801-807 it quotes Isaiah 53.7 and, by use of a second-level interpretation of the type used by churchmen, applies the words to Christ.

2. In lines 763-764 it quotes some words from the Song of Solomon 4.7, 8 and, in accordance with a second level interpretation, attributes them to Christ.

3. In lines 689-694, by linking the Wisdom of Solomon 10.10 with Genesis 28.12-15, it gives a third-level interpretation to the story of Jacob, identifying him with the righteous man to whom Wisdom showed the lovely domain of God.[9]

4. In lines 501-571 it retells the Parable of the Vineyard from Matthew 13.44,45, then offers a detailed fourth-level interpretation, with Christ represented (line 572) as saying words that in the Bible follow a different parable (Matthew 22.14) and the child (lines 573-636) explaining the parable in relation to the actualities of heaven and her new life.

The *Pearl* also contains specific hints and pointers that suggest it should be interpreted on more than one level. It opens, just as the *Commedia* does, with an allegorical passage. The *perle*, named in the first line, is referred to as *her* in the fourth line; it is described in the fifth line in terms that might apply to an actual gem, but in line 6 it is *her* again and the description (so smal, so smoþe her syde$_3$) fits a girl child better than a gem.[8b] Lines 8 and 9 continue with the pronoun *her*, but line 10 speaks of *it*. These shifts of pronoun and the ambiguous description seem as clearly intended to alert the reader to the fact that the poem is not to be interpreted strictly on a literal basis as do the leopard, the lion, and the she-wolf in Dante's first canto.

Observing Dante's caution, we will delay consideration of the second level until the first level has been determined. Let it suffice here to say that the *Pearl* seems to offer both kinds of interpretation, the churchman's and the poet's, and it draws both into a contributory relationship to the epiphany that constitutes the fourth level.

With regard to the third level the *Pearl* puts significant emphasis on moral issues as related to salvation: the sin of pride, the wretchedness of man's own will, the need for a man to become like a little child. Furthermore the poem's references to the narrator as *burne*, meaning man (397), and, in connection with the *perle*, as *juelere* (252, 265, *passim*) remind the reader that the narrator is representative (i.e., in the medieval sense, a symbol) of mankind. And these references and others work together to create the homiletic character of the poem that has been noted by numerous scholars and thus contribute to a third-level meaning intended to help all persons to understand how they can become *precios perle₃* acceptable to God.

As shown in Chapter III, the *Pearl* presents all its data through a point of view that involves an element of mystery and that indirectly challenges the reader to grasp and understand something that the narrator himself hardly understood. This something is conveyed through a revelation, an epiphany, but its consummation is announced more definitely than one would expect. In stanza 100, within a few lines of the end of the poem, the narrator says that if he had bent over to God's will and yearned more toward him, and held himself in true intent, he would have been brought to *mo* (more) of God's "mysterys." Thus the poem says clearly that the narrator did win to at least one of God's secrets and dares the reader to find the fourth-level meaning.

The multi-level type of interpretation discussed above may be unacceptable to some readers. They may dislike multifaceted symbols. They may see no point in four-level interpretations. They may want none of it.[8c]

Nevertheless, if they are interested at all, the correct classification of the *Pearl* may help them also, for even to read a veiled poem for its literal meaning requires certain safeguards and tests, which Dante suggested in *Convivio*. These safeguards supply a reasonable basis for testing assumptions made in the past about the *Pearl* and reaching safe conclusions about the literal content. So, if you are one who wants only the meaning of the story, the procedure described in the next chapter may give you what you want.

Chapter IV
Endnotes

1. "Tractus Myteriorium," I, 1, in *History and Literature of Christianity*, ed. Pierre Champagne de Labriolle, tr. Herbert Wilson (New York: Knopf, 1925), p. 243.

2. H. Flanders Dunbar, *Symbolism in Medieval Thought* (New Haven: Yale University Press, 1929), pp. 497-499.

3. Webster's *New International Dictionary of the English Language*, 2nd ed., unabridged (Springfield: G. and C. Merriam Company, 1934, rptd. with addenda, 1939, 1945, 1950, 1951), p. 68.

4. *The History of English Poetry*, ed. Richard Taylor (London, 1840), I, ccvi.

5. *Dante's Convivio*, tr. Jackson, pp. 73-75.

6. "Convivio," II, i, *Le Opere di Dante Alighiere*, p. 252. The translation is from Latham, *A Translation of Dante's Eleven Letters*, p. 194.

7. *Ibid.*

8. Caroline Gordon and Allen Tate, "Notes on Fictional Techniques," *The House of Fiction* (New York: Charles Scribner's Sons, 1950; rptd. 1960), p. 455.

8a. Eldredge helpfully summarizes some of the more striking readings of the "significance" of the pearl: "D. W. Robertson Jr, [suggests that] literally the pearl is a gem; allegorically she is a maiden in the poem, that is one of the innocent in New Jerusalem; tropologically, she is the soul that attains innocence through penance; and anagogically she is the life of innocence in the celestial city." Marie Hamilton sees the pearl as "both a maiden soul become a perle of prys and the perl of prys itself, the gem of beatitude," M. R. Stern "claims that the pearl symbolizes the ideal, the perfect unified order of divine creation." C. A. Luttrell and J. W. Earl both explore the traditional connection between "pearls" and "virginity" (specific citations for these arguments can be found in Eldredge's bibliographic essay).
    Wilson, in a rather unconvincing reading, valorizes the literal meaning – there is no reason to believe that the meaning is anything other than that the missing gem is covered by earth" (116). One perfectly good reason to believe otherwise would be that veiled poetry traditionally works simultaneously at several hermeneutical levels. We have to read against the grain of the poem's method to accept Wilson's cramped understanding of the poem's concerns.

8b. Davenport (8) and Bogdanos (9) make a similar observation regarding the play with pronouns in describing the pearl.

Wilson inexplicably contends that "the text gives no reason for supposing, as many commentators on the poem have done, that the narrator is 'actually' referring to a girl; 'rounde,' 'smal,' and 'smoþe' are immediately comprehensible adjectives for a pearl..." (117). Wilson disposes with the problem of pronoun ambiguity by blissfully ignoring it.

8c.   Mystification is part of the generic expectation that a reader brings to "veiled poetry." Hence, when a critic like Hendrix anachronistically uses Fish's categories of "self-satisfying works [that] affirm rational and discursive structures" versus "self-consuming works" that "subvert" them (459), his argument tends to beg the question. Mystification and polysemous levels of meaning are generically associated with veiled poetry—in other words, veiled poetry satisfies the reader's generic expectations precisely by teasing him or her through withholding the full meaning of the text.

9.   See note on line 690 in *Pearl*, ed. Gordon, pp. 70-71.

CHAPTER V

A LOVELY LITTLE GIRL SHARING GOD'S KNOWLEDGE

Level 1

The key to understanding veiled poetry, as Dante demonstrated in *Convivio*, is close, analytical reading that takes into consideration all the ways in which meaning may be conveyed. He specifically states that one should consider "construction of language which concerns the grammarian," the order of discourse "which pertains to the orator," and the rhythm of the poem's parts "which pertains to the musician."[1] Dante thus makes plain the importance of considering diction and sentence structure, imagery and tone, organization, movement, the inter-relationship and congruence of parts – including all those schemata, figures, tropes, and other elements and devices that medieval students grouped under *grammatica* and *rhetorica*.

The study of the "construction of language" includes the discovery of the direct and implied meanings of images, symbols, allusions; the study of "the order of discourse" includes the finding of meanings implied by the position of a statement or image in relation to other statements or images and to the whole; the study of "the rhythm [harmony] of parts" implies the consideration of hints and changes of tone – recognition of the fact that the tone and meaning (direct or implied) of one part may throw light on the meaning (direct or implied) of another part. And all these things, Dante says, "can meetly be perceived...by him who looks closely."[2]

The application of this method obviously makes large demands on the reader: it requires, first, awareness of the difficulty; second, knowledge of medieval education and thought; and, third, time for examining, looking below the surface and between the lines, thinking, testing, and re-evaluating where necessary.

Nevertheless Richard Morris, first editor of the *Pearl*, apparently saw no difficulty. Instead of looking for implications and hints, he took the poem to be crude and paid attention only to the surface. Instead of trying to resolve contradictions through study of the congruence of the whole, he was ready to assume childish lack of sense. Instead of working slowly and carefully, he worked fast. Yet, because of his long career and industry, because of the overwhelming prestige of the nineteenth-century philological movement, in which he shared both as co-founder of the Early English Text Society and as editor and author, perhaps also because of the piecemeal and incomplete way in which modern criticism and revision have proceeded, his interpretation of the *Pearl*, after going unquestioned for forty years, still underlies the orthodox interpretation and even controls the dissenting interpretations at some critical points.

Errors in definition of words have been found and corrected; for example, *rot* (line 26), meaning rot, defined by Morris as root; *woȝe* (151), peril, defined by Morris as path; *byte* (355), bite, defined by Morris as fierce. Likewise errors in etymology have been pointed out; for example, *sengeley* (8), from Old French *sengle*, but said by Morris to be from Old English *singallice*; and *spenned* (53), from Old Norse *spenna*, but according to Morris from Old English *spannan*. Also some of his readings of particular passages have been swept away; for example, 359-360, which Morris translated, "For to ruin, or make foolish, grieve or to soothe,/ All lies in him to order and doom," Gordon has shown to mean, "For, though you may lament or rave, or mourn and conceal it, (yet) all lies in God's power to dispose and judge."[3]

Though the whole view of the *Pearl* taken by Morris has been challenged by some modern scholars, the initial assumptions made by Morris, the rule-of-thumb decisions set up on the spur of the moment as necessary steps to a scientific view of the grammar and dialect of the poem (Morris's chief interests) have never been thoroughly examined or analyzed as a group, in relation to each other and to the different interpretations of the poem. It therefore becomes necessary here, as a preliminary to establishing the literal meaning of the poem, to look at these assumptions as objectively as possible, without prejudgment as to their correctness or incorrectness, but with full recognition that they are assumptions, and to determine what evidence or what good reasons there may be for maintaining, rejecting, or modifying them.

The first assumption made by Morris is that the man and the child in *The Pearl* are real people, (1) not abstractions or personifications and (2) not fictitious creations. He never admits that this is an assumption and never presents any facts or reasoning to support it – in fact, he does not discuss it at all. It was first questioned by Schofield, who claimed the girl to be a personification, and defended by Coulton, who directed his remarks against the idea that the child personified pure virginity and made his point by citing lines in the poem which showed clearly that the girl had lived on earth, died, been mourned, and was now in heaven. The implications of the poem are on Coulton's and Morris' side, for the very fact that the names of the man and girl are withheld suggests the desire to shield real people, just as Dante in the *Vita Nuova* shields the sympathetic lady who consoled him after the loss of Beatrice by withholding her name and likewise withholds the last name of Beatrice to prevent her being positively identified. The other aspect of the assumption – that the characters are real, not fictitious – was not discussed by Schofield and Coulton, and, since it is related to the next point, will be discussed below.

Morris' second assumption is that the "I" who speaks in the poem is the author, and this in turn rests on another unacknowledged assumption – the idea that the Middle Ages were the childhood of the race and that the writers of that time were obviously too naive to think of representing someone else as "I". Gordon defended this assumption on the grounds that "the purely fictitious 'I'..., a first person feigned as narrator who had no existence outside the imagination of the real author," had probably not yet appeared in the fourteenth century, but then cancels his own argument by referring to Sir John Mandeville, the fictitious "I" of the *Travels*. He also disregards the fact that the "dramatic I," – the use of "I" by a character

56

in story, play, history, letter, or pretended document – was firmly established in medieval theory and practice.[4] In many medieval rhetorics, beginning with the Venerable Bede and coming on down through the centuries, poetry is divided into three kinds, the dramatic, the narrative, and the mixed. The dramatic, Bede says, is that in which the characters (*personae*) "are presented as speaking without the intervention of the poet, as in tragedies and fables, for drama is called in Latin *fabula*."

> In this kind is written "Quo te Moeri pedes? an quo via ducit in urbem?" as also among ourselves the Song of Songs, where the voice of Christ and of the Church are clearly found to alternate without the writer's intervention. That is *exegematicon*, or narrative, in which the poet himself speaks without the intervention of any *persona*, as three books of the Georgics and the first part of the fourth, as well as the poems of Lucretius and others like them....*Coenon* or mixed, is the kind in which the poet himself speaks and also the *personae* are presented as speaking. So are written the *Iliad* and *Odyssey* of Homer, the *Aeneid* of Vergil,...[5]

If this does not dispose of the matter, consider the fact that Petronius' *Satyricon*, in which Eucolpius is chief character and narrator, was known to the Middle Ages; also *The Golden Ass*, which is told in the first person; and *Aethiopica*, in which Calasiris tells a part of the story in the first person. Moreover the Middle Ages were familiar with Ovid's imaginary letters written in the first person by Ariadne, Cleopatra, and many another, and also they had their own imaginary letters like the one from Balteser, the son of the King of "Sarsyn," as well as their forged documents like the pretended autobiography of Pope Celestine.[6] There are also the miracle plays with every character speaking as "I," the many poems and stories in which there are long dramatic speeches in the first person, not to mention Sir John Mandeville and poems like "The Dream of the Rood," in which Christ's Cross speaks as "I."[7]

Considering all the facts, it is ridiculous to suppose that the fictitious "I" was unknown. Furthermore, the handling of viewpoint in *The Pearl* is a technical achievement, comparable in its way to that of Henry James in *The Ambassadors*, as was suggested in Chapter III. Such exploration of the narrator's mind does not preclude the conclusion that the narrator is the author, for Dante was able in similar fashion to explore his own mind in the

Divine Comedy, but it does seem likely that such exploration could be done with less distortion and difficulty by a perceptive third person than by the possessor of the explored mind.

If the "I" of *The Pearl* is not the author, the first-person narration might have been chosen for any one or more of several reasons: because a vision of heaven or hell is a personal and individual experience and sounds more natural and authentic in the first person; or because the visions of St. John in Revelation and of the Prophets in the Old Testament are in the first person, as is also the vision of St. Paul, which was accepted as authentic in the Middle Ages; or because the author of *The Pearl* based his work on an actual first-person narrative, written or dictated by the person who had the vision; or because the identity of the narrator had to be withheld and the use of "I" seemed the easiest and most effective way to withhold the name without emphasizing the fact that it was withheld.

The third assumption is that the narrator and the girl are persons of modest background and position, and this is based primarily on the preceding assumption that the narrator is the author and the further assumption that the girl is his daughter. Implied but not stated by Morris, it is developed in some detail by ten Brink and Gollancz in their imaginary biographies of the author. In Gollancz' view the poet's father was probably connected, in some official capacity, with a family of high rank, and the poet was brought up in some great castle, educated at a monastic school or perhaps at one of the universities, and was attached to the household of some nobleman, who became his generous patron.[8] Gordon supports this view in a milder form. The author, he says, may have had a monastic education, shows interest in the arts and aristocratic activities of his day, and perhaps was a chaplain in an aristocratic household.[9]

The language of the poem, however, suggests a much higher rank for both man and child. Lines 489-492 suggest that in the man's thought the girl might have reason to claim the rank of "countes, damysel,...oþer elleȝ a lady of lasse aray." It may be objected that he is talking about rank in heaven, not on earth; however, since such rank would not be recognized in heaven and since he is a man of earth, unable to think in terms of heaven's society, his remarks may very well be interpreted as reflecting earth's standards.

Furthermore, in another passage (361), he speaks of her as "þat damyselle," a title of respect applicable even to a king's daughter, and the girl herself gives evidence of aristocratic nurture and training; for instance, in lines 235-238, and elsewhere, she shows the courtesy and easy manners of one born to high position. He also is called "gente" (noble), thus suggesting that he is a nobleman.

The first line of the poem says that the girl was pleasing enough to delight a prince; and this reference to an earthly prince is made memorable and emphatic by the closing stanza of the poem with its reference to the need for pleasing another prince, the Lord of heaven. The Middle Ages, with their emphasis on rank and protocol, would not mention the word *prince* without the intention of conveying an idea of royalty; and a concept of royalty, with a contrast between earthly royalty and heavenly royalty, stands at the very heart of the poem. Johnson, in his discussion of imagery, emphasized the psychological effect of the idea of royalty on the author and points out that royalty is "consistently associated" with the poem's images of light and jewelry.[10] The poem's excessive care in withholding any sort of clue to the man's identity may be another indication that he was a man of very high rank.

That the child died before she was two years old is Morris' fourth assumption. The basis for this assumption is l. 483 of the poem:

þou lyfed not two ȝer in oure þede,

which Morris took to mean, "She was only two years old when she died," and Gollancz translated as follows: "thou livedst not two years in our land."[11] Neither gave the slightest recognition to the fact that the line might have a different meaning, and neither mentioned any discrepancy between the child's appearance and behavior and her supposed age.

Schofield raised the first objection, pointing out that the child "does not demean herself as a babe of two years,"[12] and Coulton made the first rebuttal.[13] "It would be difficult," he said, "to name any book medieval or modern that fulfils" Schofield's implied requirement (i.e., that a child in a poem or story should act like a real child). This rebuttal is hardly convincing, for the point at issue was not the realistic or unrealistic coloring of the child's portrait, but the obvious discrepancy between the appearance of the child and her supposed age. As Conley pointed out,

> A child of two or thereabout in the pre-Wordsworthian era with which we are dealing, besides being a symbol of innocence, was also, as even now, a symbol of irrationality. In *The Romaunt of the Rose* we find (Robinson, p. 668, ll. 400-402); "She [Elde] had nothing hirsilf to lede,/ Ne wit ne pithe in hir hold,/ More than a child of two years old."[14]

Coulton offered a second argument. "Pearl's behavior in heaven," he said, "can scarcely be more inconsistent with her life than Beatrice's is;..."[15] Osgood echoed this argument, saying, Pearl was "changed, like Beatrice, by the glory of her blessed condition."[16] However, this line of rebuttal also seems doubtful since the child is portrayed as obviously older than two (but still a child), whereas Beatrice is not presented as changed in age or size but merely as glorified:

> Under her veil and beyond the stream she seemed to surpass her former self more than she did others when on earth.[17]

Osgood offers a further line of thought to support this view: she is portrayed "in maturity" for theological reasons. He then cites St. Augustine to the effect that at the resurrection each of the saved will rise in a state of ultimate perfection, "which is in the youthful age, at which time the movement of growth terminates, and from which the movement of decrease begins," that is, at about the age of thirty.[18]

The trouble with this argument is twofold: (1) the child is not portrayed as a mature woman of thirty; on the contrary, she is a *faunt* (child);[18a] (2) since the day of Resurrection has not yet come, the bodies of the saved have not yet risen and will not, according to the Bible, until the end of the world. In the meantime the spirits of the dead, though not having bodies, appear in the semblance of their earthly bodies, according to medieval belief, and thus may be recognized by those who knew them on earth, as Dante in his vision recognized many he saw in hell, purgatory, and heaven. He specifically mentions seeing children in limbo and in heaven.[19]

So this line of thought was quietly dropped, and the whole weight of the argument was placed on the idea that the maturity of Pearl (still asserted in spite of the descriptive details furnished by the poem) represents a "convention," a "concession," Osgood said, "for the sake of verisimilitude in the dialogue."[20] This supposed convention is supported by the supposed fact that Boccaccio in *Olympia* likewise portrayed his young daughter, an infant, as an adult. Further investigation, however, showed that Boccaccio's daughter did not die as an infant; in a letter to Petrarch, Boccaccio says she was five and a half the last time he saw her;[21] and a period of time (at least a few months, perhaps longer) elapsed between that time and the time of her death. In the poem Boccaccio says she looks older than when he saw her last – that she looks old enough for marriage[22] – but when we remember that child-marriage was customary in the Middle Ages, the remark does not mean that he thought she looked like a full-grown woman.

So virtually all the evidence to support the idea of a dead two-year-old appearing as an adult in heaven dropped away; and Gollancz in 1921 met the situation by crediting the change in both Pearl and Boccaccio's daughter to "theological fancy"[23] on the part of the respective authors – an idea not in keeping with the medieval concept of theology as a science. Due to some oversight, however, Gordon was still able to say (erroneously):

> Olympia is known to have lived on earth, and to have died as
> an infant, and, like the Pearl, in her glorified state she speaks
> as an adult and as one having authoritative knowledge.[24]

In actuality, of course, there seems to be no real reason for supposing either Olympia or the Pearl died as an infant.

The interpretation of l. 483 by Morris resulted from his giving to *pede*, meaning nation or country, an extended poetic meaning, "land of the living," so that the whole line could be interpreted to mean, "You did not live two years in the land of the living." Obviously this is not the only possible meaning. *Oure pede* might mean "our country," as opposed to a foreign country, and then the line would mean, "You did not live two years in our country [before you were taken into a different country]." Or it might mean "our land" in the sense of the everyday world of our secular interests and activities, as opposed to the world of the religious (i.e., the monk and the nun). Thus St. Bernard of Clairvaux spoke of "people in the world" as distinguished from "people in a Religious House,"[25] and likewise a common distinction was made among the clergy between those living "in the world" and those who lived in monastic seclusion. So, also, there was a distinction made between the world outside the walls of monastery and "the holy land" inside the walls.

Nothing in the *Pearl* implies that the child was taken to a foreign country before her death, but here is much that implies that she was a religious. Sister Mary Madeleva called attention to the fact that the beatific condition enjoyed by the girl – her place as Bride of the spotless Lamb – is the hope of every religious and that the heaven portrayed is "the heaven of virgins." Such position, she believed, is "dependent on deliberate choice, postulating deliberate renunciation." Thus, and in other passages, Sister Mary gives her belief that the girl was a member of a religious community.[26]

That the author of the *Pearl* intended to suggest that the city he portrayed (985-1152) was the city of God in the third heaven is probably shown by his mention of the Virtues (1126), regarded by St. Gregory, Hugh of St. Victor, St. Bernard, as well as the English mystic, Richard Rolle, as the third order of angels, hence the guardians of the third heaven.[27] That he intended to portray the girl as a religious is clearly shown by his description of her dress (197-204) and crown (205-208) and the details of the procession in which she marched (1096-1108). According to the medieval view, authentically stated by Vincent de Beauvais, the virgins in heaven enjoy three special honors: they wear a special crown, they sing a special song before the throne that no one else can sing, and they are led by the Lamb himself.[28] These prerogatives are described as follows in *Hali Meidenhad*:

> ...in the grace of maidenhood and in its virtue, none may follow him, nor the blessed maiden, the lady of angels, and honour of maidens, but maidens only. And hence is their attire so bright and sheen beyond all others, that they always go next to God, whithersoever he turneth. And they are all crowned that enjoy bliss in heaven, with champions' crowns. But maidens have beyond that, which is common to all alike, a diadem [*Ms. gerlondesche*] shining sheener than the sun: "Aureola" it is called in the Latin language. It is not for human speech to tell of the nature of the flowers that are drawn thereon, nor of the gemstones therein.[29]

In the *Pearl* (1095-1116) the child walks in the procession of virgins, all dressed alike in glittering white, each wearing a crown

> Hi₃e pynakled of cler quyt perle
> Wyth flurted flowre₃ perfet vpon.   (207-208)

At their head walked God the Son, in the guise of a Lamb, and all were his brides.

The fact that the child is thus portrayed as one of the virgins in heaven has created a crux for those who accept the Victorian interpretation and believe that she died before she was two, and they have tried to get out of the difficulty by proposing that, even though she could not have renounced the world and become a religious before she was two and therefore was not a virgin in the religious sense, she might have been accepted among the virgins and walked with them because she was an innocent. They support this proposition by pointing out that the Innocents slain by King Herod also march in the heavenly procession and that the little "clergeon" in the Prioress' Tale by Chaucer, a "martir, souded to virginitee," also marches there.[30] But they overlook the fact that the Innocents as well as the clergeon got their place of honor in the heavenly procession through martyrdom, that the Innocents were regarded as truly martyrs by the Church, and that the medieval pictures of the New Jerusalem include three main groups in the heavenly procession: the martyrs, the virgins, and the holy teachers or confessors. Each of these, martyr, virgin, or teacher, got his place in the procession by giving his all for Christ, and it is not possible to gain a place among them – the sainted ones – with less.

So, when Elizabeth Hart,[31] seeking to show that the girl in the *Pearl* might win her place among the virgins merely by dying while she was an innocent baby, argues that a kind of "association of the Holy Innocents with the procession" in medieval times would permit this inclusion, she was not speaking with the intellectual precision that characterizes medieval theology.

The question, then, arises: could the child have been placed in a convent before she was two? The answer is yes – at least children were placed in convents at a very early age, sometimes in infancy, the records say,[32] and there is one specific instance where a child is definitely stated to have been placed in a convent before she was two. This was Eleana, or Alienor, putative daughter of King Edward I, who was placed before her second birthday in the convent at Amesbury, where her half-sister, Mary, was a nun.[33] Infants, on being placed in convent or monastery, might be regarded as dedicated to the monastic life, but they would probably be expected or required at a later time to make their personal commitment. When could such commitment be made? At the age at which a person might be regarded as a "citizen of heaven," to use Boccaccio's phrase. This was the age of accountability, which might vary with the child, but would come somewhere between the ages of five and seven. At least the Church regarded seven as the age of accountability,[34] but there are known instances of children taking their vows between five and seven. Mary, King Edward I's daughter, mentioned above, is said to have taken the veil at the age of five.[35]

How old was the child in the poem at the time of her death? The Victorian interpreters, without bothering about her earthly age or the logic and congruence of the poem, apparently pictured her as a mature person; at least the drawing by Holman Hunt, for Gollancz' 1891 edition, gives her the face and figure of a woman of twenty or more. In arriving at this picture they were probably influenced by the severity, logic, and intelligence of the child's remarks, without taking into consideration the fact that these qualities represented the medieval idea of beatitude – the complete knowledge that comes even to a child who looks upon the face of God. Perhaps also they were influenced to some extent by the crude illustrations that accompany the manuscript, for these picture her as young lady, probably in her teens; but the drawings were made after the manuscript was written about 1400, some thirty years after the composition of the poem, and they do not furnish any sure evidence that the artist had read the poem, for they vary from the text in many ways.

At any rate the picture given both by the Victorians and the manuscript illustrations disregards some concrete details given in the poem and their implications. She is a child (*faunt*, 161), a little queen (1147), so small so attractively slender (190); in her discussion of her reward in heaven she classes herself with the innocent children (613-636); she infers that she did not live long enough to do any good works; she states specifically that she died while she was "ful ȝong & tender of age" (412); and the man says that at the time of her death she did not know the Lord's Prayer or the Apostles' Creed (485). She is described as being dressed like a grown woman in a *bleaunt* of fine white linen or silk (a loose surcoat trimmed with pearls, with openings extending from the waist to the lowest hem) over a *cortel* of the same material (a close-fitting gown reaching from neck to feet) visible at the sleeves and through the openings (197-204); but this does not indicate that she was an adult. In medieval times children, when they had outgrown their babyhood, were dressed like grown-ups.

The general particulars of her description make clear that she was a child; the fact that she did not know the Lord's Prayer indicates that she was under seven, for the teaching of the Lord's Prayer would not have been delayed beyond that age; and her commitment to a nun's life means that she had reached the age of accountability. In all probability, then, she died between the ages of five and seven.

Morris' fifth assumption is that the narrator was the father of the child; and this seems the most likely explanation of the intense love and grief that the man feels for the girl. But there are complications not immediately explainable, as Schofield and others have shown. First, the man never calls the girl his daughter, and she never calls him father. In Schofield's words, "the poet takes pains never anywhere to state that the Pearl is the dreamer's daughter."[36] Second, the man, when he first sees the girl, is not sure of her identity; though he says, "I knew hyr wel, I hade sen hyr ere" (164) and later adds that the longer he looked at her, the better he knew her, still he has to ask, "Art þou my perle...?" (242) These two points suggest (1) that if she is his daughter, there is some reason why neither she nor he can openly admit it and (2) that her appearance has changed to some degree since he last saw her, thus implying that they had been separated before her death and she had grown and altered in that interval, as small children do when they change from toddlers into little girls.

Gollancz once suggested that "perhaps she was a love-child, hence his *privy* pearl,"[37] echoing the phrase used in line 24 of the poem. This suggestion has been indignantly denied by others, but it accords with the poem's implications. In itself, however, it does not explain the fact that both avoid admitting their relationship; as Schofield points out, Olympia was an illegitimate child, but Boccaccio did not hesitate to admit his relationship to her, and in his poem about her she is represented as calling him father.[38]

Individuals, of course, might vary in their sensitiveness to admitting such a relationship; but the failure in the *Pearl* ever–first, middle, or last, in a poem much longer than Boccaccio's–to name the relationship and the constant maintenance of a sort of emotional tension between the man and the child suggests a tie that held the two together and also kept them apart.

The man speaks of "my wrange" (15), meaning "my sin," as Sister Mary Vincent Hillmann interprets it,[39] and also of his grieving for her alone at night (243); and once (380) he alludes to meeting her "by stok oþer ston" (i.e., by the wayside, as Schofield translated it). "Would a *father* ever speak of meeting his own daughter 'by stock or stone,' and nowhere else?" Schofield asks.[40] The answer is yes–if the child were illegitimate, if the relationship could never be acknowledged, and if the father's only chance of seeing his child was what would appear to be an accidental meeting by the wayside.

Imagine such a relationship existing between a great nobleman, the son or grandson of a king, conscious of his rank and his blood, and a little girl, supposed to be the daughter of another–a relationship that was not acknowledged during her life and never could be. Then imagine the situation presented in the poem: the father sees his child in eternity; each knows the other and each knows the true relationship; but neither can speak about it. Hence the tension, the effort to avoid any word that would be wrong in view of what had already happened and could never be altered.

Illicit relationships were common, especially among the aristocracy, in the thirteenth and fourteenth centuries. King Edward I in his youth had an illicit affair with the Countess of Gloucester.[41] Thomas, Earl of Lancaster's wife eloped with another man.[42] Queen Isabella, wife of Edward II, deserted her husband to live with her love, Mortimer. Edward III had his Alice Perrers and John of Gaunt, his Catherine Roet.[43] Two princesses at the court of Philip the Fair, in France, were taken in adultery.[44] Even the churchmen had their loves; for example, the Bishop of Lichfield, a favorite of Edward I, was accused of living in adultery.[45] A poet, writing early in the century, summarized the situation as follows:

The tenþe comaundement ys, "by þy lyfe
Couete nat þy neghburs wyfe."
And þys ys now a comun synne
þat many one fallyn ynne,

> For almost hyt ys euery-whore
> A gentyl man haþ a wyfe and a hore;
> And wyues have now comunly
> here husbondys and a ludby.[46]

Illicit loves might be clothed in the poetic beauty and glamour of the courtly love tradition, but there was also a tragic side evident in the fate of illegitimate children and the punishment sometimes meted out to women caught in adultery and their seducers.

The conclusions reached in our re-examination of the *Pearl* may be summarized briefly as follows:

1. The man and the child are represented as real persons, not personifications.

2. The narrator, though every detail in the poem is presented from his viewpoint, is probably not the author.

3. The poem, without directly saying so, indicates that the narrator is a prince and that the child has some unspecified connection with royalty.

4. The child was placed in a convent before she was two years old and died before she was seven.

5. She was an illegitimate child, the unacknowledged daughter of the narrator.

Some further conclusions may be drawn from details of setting. The "erbere" or garden in which the child is buried is not a cemetery: there are flowers and herbs and peartrees, but not a single plant or tree is mentioned that would be associated with graveyards. Since the flowers mentioned are

> Gilofre, gyngure, & gromylyoun,
> & pyonys powdered ay betwene   (43, 44)

some have argued that the whole picture is conventional, literary, and unreal, for ginger does not grow in England. But the *English Dialect Dictionary* shows *ginger* to have been used as a name for some plants native to England (the biting stone-crop, the crooked yellow stonecrop, and tansy), and Sister Mary Madeleva has suggested that this may well be "the herb-garden of a monastery, fair and fragrant with such plants as one would find there:..."[47] There is a mound over the child's grave (41, 62, 1172, 1205), with the flowers shading it, but no monument or marker is mentioned in the poem or shown in the illustration that pictures the mound.

The flowers imply that the child has been dead for at least a few months – long enough for the flowers to grow on her grave – and the burial in a garden suggests some sort of difficulty in obtaining holy burial for her. The unconventional place of burial, together with the lack of monument or markcr, underlines the father's grief, frustration, and anger at his inability to help his daughter while alive or to give her honorable burial inside a church or churchyard with monument and memorial. These things were very important in the medieval world.

The time of his visit to her grave is "in Auguste in a hy$_3$ seysoun," (39) and some have thought this to be the feast of the Assumption of the Virgin; others, the feast of the First Fruits, called Lammas. Because the poem mentions the cutting of grain (40), Gordon takes it to be Lammas,[48] which is doubly appropriate (1) because the child says that the Virgins (of whom she was one) were redeemed as first fruits due to God (893-894) and (2) because in the fourteenth century Lammas was the principal feast "whan þer is gret pardon of plenyr remyssyon, for to þurchasyn grace, mercy, & for$_3$evenes"[49] and the man of the *Pearl* found his lost child and his pardon that day.

The conclusions reached here do not require any large alterations in the story-line of the *Pearl* as understood by present-day adherents of the orthodox interpretation; but they do eliminate the most troublesome and unreasonable element in the older view (the difference between the girl's appearance and her supposed age) and they also add a richness of substance and meaning in keeping with the view of those who find elaborate and complex beauty in the imagery and workmanship of the poem.

The literal meaning of the *Pearl*, if we keep in mind the conclusions and implications given above, may be summarized, in the main, in the terms of Moorman's analysis.[50] The poem begins with the man visiting his child's grave. Struggling with his grief and resentment, he goes into a trance ("slepyng-sla$_3$te"59), in which his spirit is separated from his body. In this state, then, for the divine vision of a person still living on earth "is restricted to the soul , and involves as a pre-requisite the temporary abstraction of the

68

soul from the processes of the body,"[51] he is able to experience the miracle described in the main part of the poem.

First, the man feels that he has entered a world of marvels (61-160). He finds himself inside a shaft of intensely brilliant light, with no apparent source, bounded by strange hills with "relusaunt" crystal cliffs. This light streams down on the garden where his body still lies and transforms all that it touches.

The man seems to move without effort through the surrounding woodland and well-watered valleys and then along the banks of a stream, where everything is made bright and precious by the reflected light. But all the while he has never left the garden, for in his conversation with the girl she refers to her grave "in his þis garden" (260), where they are standing.[52]

The scholars who have taken this to be a representation of the earthly paradise seem obviously misled by their desire to interpret the details of the poem as "conventional"; for the picture is highly original, as Patch pointed out in The Other World,[53] and, though the hills and the crystal cliffs belong to heaven, the rest of the picture (37-44, 101-144) is a down-to-earth English place –, woodland, fields, hedgerows, many streams, and a monastic garden with herbs and peartrees adjacent to a brook dammed up to make a series of pools – beautiful in itself, but made inexpressibly beautiful and precious by God's light.

In this setting, across the brook, below a shining crystal cliff, he sees a girl. Her world is one of light – not of reflected light – for she herself has inner brightness. He is afraid to speak to her, but she takes off her crown, waves to him, and greets him lightly. At this point (241) the colloquy begins. "Art þou my perle...?" the man says, thus revealing his earthly point of view. The tone and substance of the girl's answer "reveals the gulf between them": "Sir, ȝe haf your tale mysetente,..."(257).

> He asks pity; she demands full understanding. Neither can grant the other's request or acknowledge the other's point of view.[54]

In Moorman's analysis the debate that follows is divided into four parts. First, the narrator blames the girl for her happiness while he has been miserable and questions her right to the high place she holds in the heavenly hierarchy. The girl replies by citing the Parable of the Vineyard and ends by emphasizing the differences between his point of view and hers. He says her "tale is vnresounable" (590). Thus her first attempt to teaching him fails. He has failed even to recognize her point of view and continues to advance earthly standards in opposition to hers.

Second, the girl explains "carefully and in detail the relationship between grace and merit and the place of the innocent...in heaven." She ends by admonishing him to forsake his earthly standards:

> I rede þe forsake þe worlds wode
> And porchase þy perle maskelles.   (743-744)

> The point of her remark...is that the difference in standards between heaven and earth is such that the achieving of the pearl (here plainly symbolizing beatitude) demands a complete renunciation of wealth and hence earthly standards of wealth. That the narrator is beginning to see the point of the girl's remarks is evident in that, for the first time in the poem, he himself seems to perceive the nature and width of the [stream] which separates them:...[55]

Third, the maiden tries to help him by describing Christ's sufferings in the Old Jerusalem and her own happiness in the New Jerusalem. Again, her point is the same, that heavenly standards are not earthly standards, but this time she deals directly with the paradox which lies at the root of the narrator's difficulty:

> Alþa$_3$ oure corses in clotte$_3$ clynge,...
> We þur$_3$outly hauen cnawyng:...
> þe Lombe vus glade$_3$,...   (857-861)

Upon hearing this statement, the narrator comes closer than before to a true and lasting understanding of their differences:

> I am bot mokke & mul among,
> & þou so ryche a reken rose,...   (905-906)

But "he cannot resist asking a favor; he would see the New Jerusalem himself."[56] Still the earthly point of view.

Fourth, the vision of the New Jerusalem provides "the final step in the process" by which the narrator "comes to understand the meaning of death." Through God's grace the barriers between heaven and earth are removed,

and the man stands on a hillslope near the source of the brook that flows
through the garden, and looks directly into God's city.

> ...the separation between earthly and heavenly standards of
> value is complete; there is no need of earthly light or even of
> earthly religious forms...The climax...comes when the poet
> perceives, with his own eyes, his "lyttel quene" (1147)...among
> her peers, happy again "wiþ lyf" (1146),...and all his doubts
> disappear. In an ecstasy, he wishes to cross over to her but is
> awakened from his dream and finds himself again in [the]
> garden, his head upon the grave.[57]

The object presented and studied in this poem, Moorman says, is the
mind of the narrator. Hence the better we understand that mind, the more
we get from the poem. To see the implications of personal tragedy in the
poem—illicit love, adultery, the illegitimate child that can never be
acknowledged, but is greatly loved, the forced separation of the man and
child (dragged apart, the poem says), the rejection of the child by the mother
and the placing of her in a convent, the estrangement from the mother so
deep that it is impossible for either man or child to mention her when they
meet in the vision, the child's death and burial without honor, the man's
desperation and self-blame—all this contributes not only to a greater
understanding of the tormented mind of the narrator, but also to our
perception and understanding of some powerful religious ideas that
characterized and motivated a long, fertile period of European history.

CHAPTER V
Endnotes

1. *Dante's Convivio*, tr. Jackson, pp. 180, 268-269.

2. *Idem*. In the *Convivio* Dante offers guidance to readers in a playful, ironical way. He first addresses, not his reader, but one of his poems says, in effect, "You are dense [that is, highly compact in language] and difficult [that is, you contain such important information, not generally known]. So, when the reader says, 'I can't understand you,' don't despair. Tell him to look closely at the quality and meaning of your language, your bodily arrangement, and the harmony of your parts, and he will easily perceive how beautiful you are [and also understand what you're saying]."

3. *Early English Alliterative Poems*, "Glossarial Index," pp. 185, 213, 132, 190, 194; "Notes," p. 107; and *Pearl*, ed. Gordon, p. 59.

4. Gordon, p. xiv. Milroy points out that even if we accept "Gordon's point that the 'purely fictitious I' had probably not yet appeared," the issue seems to be a "red herring" because one could always argue that "*Pearl* might be its first occurrence and that in the work of a poet of extraordinary imaginative and intellectual power" (208) – literary conventions should be used cautiously as pieces of evidence when discussing works of enormously original imaginative power.

5. *Grammatici latini*, ed. H. Keil (Leipzig, 1870-1880), vii, 259, quoted in translation by Charles Sears Baldwin, *Medieval Rhetoric and Poetic* (New York: Macmillan, 1928), pp. 131-132.

6. *The Vercelli Book*, ed. George Philip Knapp, (New York: Columbia University Press, 1932), pp. 61-65.

7. *Ibid*.

8. *Pearl*, ed. Gollancz (1921), pp. xli-xiii.

9. *Pearl*, ed. Gordon, p. xiii.

10. Johnson, *loc. cit.*, pp. 171-172.

11. Morris, *loc. cit.*, p. 15; Gollancz, *Pearl*, (1921), p. 43.

12. Schofield, "The Nature and Fabric of *The Pearl*," *loc. cit.*, p. 167.

13. Coulton, *loc. cit.*, p. 41.

14. Conley, *loc. cit.*, p. 341, note 43.

15. Coulton, p. 41.

16. *The Pearl*, ed. Osgood, p. xxx.

17. "Purgatory," xxxi, 82-84; Huse's translation, p. 314.

18. *The Pearl*, ed. Osgood, pp. xxv-xxvi, citing St. Augustine, *De Civ. Dei*, xxii, 14-15, Patr. Lat., xli, 776.

18a. Similarly, Malcolm Andrew drawing upon the Middle English use of the word "faunt" argues that the Maiden is a "literal" rather than an "allegorical figure" (4). Of course, in some sense the alternative implied by that formulation is a false one – the literal maiden simultaneously sustains an allegorical signifcance.

19. "Inferno," iv, 28-30, and "Paradiso," xxxii, 40-84, *Le Opere di Dante*, pp. 5 and 150-151. The translation is from Huse, *op cit.*, pp. 22-23 and 473-474.

20. Osgood, p. xxv.

21. Quoted and translated from *Le Lettere edite e inedite di Messer Giovanni Boccaccio*, ed. F. Corazzini (Florence, 1977), by Gollancz in *Pearl* (1921), 252-255.

22. "Olympia," Boccaccio's XIVth Eclogue, in Gollancz's *Pearl*, pp. 264-265.

23. *Idem.*, p. 248.

24. Gordon, p. xxxv.

25. *Sancti Bernardi Opera*, ed. J. Leclercq et al. (Rome, Editiones Cistercienses, 1958), II.

26. Sister M. Madeleva, *op cit.*, pp. 152-154, 178.

27. Third Order of Angels, St. Gregory, Hugh of St. Victor and Richard Rolle.

28. Vincent de Beauvais, *The Virgins have Three Special Hours.*

29. *Hali Meidenhad*, an alliterative homily of the thirteenth century, ed. F. J. Furnivall, revised by Oswald Cockayne, EETS O. S. 58 (London, 1922), 31.

30. *The Poetical Works of Chaucer*, ed. F. N. Robinson (Boston: Houghton Mifflin, 1933), pp. 195-196.

31. "The Heaven of Virgins," MLN, 42 (1927), pp. 113-116.

32. E. G., Princess Mary, DNB, VII, 38; and Gertrude the Great, in Sister M. Madeleva, *op. cit.*, p. 50.

33. Francis Lancelott, *The Queens of England and Their Times* (New York: D. Appleton, 1856), I, 164.

34. *Codex Iuris Canonici Pii X Pontificis Maximi* Westminster, Maryland, 1954), Canon 88, Secion 3.

35. DNB, VII, 38. Lancelott says she entered the convent at the age of five, but took the veil at the age of seven (*op. cit.*, I 140).

36. Schofield, "The Nature and Fabric of *The Pearl*," *loc. cit.*, 160.

37. *The Cambridge History of English Literature*, (Cambridge: The University Press, vol I, 1911; rptd., 1960), I, 331.

38. "Olympia," *loc. cit.*, p. 262, line 40.

39. Hillman, "Some Debatable Words," MLN 60 (1945), 243.

40. Schofield, "Symbolism, Allegory, and Autobiography in *The Pearl*," *loc. cit.*, 663-664.

41. DNB, "Edward I," XVII, 20.

42. DNB, "Thomas, 2nd Earl of Lancaster," OVI, 151.

43. DNB, XXIX, 65-66.

44. *Ibid.*, XVII, 68; XVIV, 426.

45. *Biographie universelle (michaud) Ancienne et Moderne* (Paris, 1854-64), XXVI, 560.

46. "Walter Langton," DNB, XXXII, p. 130.

47. Robert of Brunne's *Handiynge Synne*, A. D., 1303, Pat I, ed. Frederick J. Furnivall, EETS O. S. 119 (London, 1901), pp. 103-104.

48. Sister M. Madeleva, *op cit.*, pp. 99-100.

49. *Pearl*, ed. Gordon, p. 47, note 39.

50. *The Book of Margery Kempe*, ed. Sanford Meech, E. E. T. S., O. S. 212 (London, 1940), p. 170.

51. Moorman, "The Role of the Narrator in *Pearl*," *loc. cit.*, pp. 77-81.

52. A. B. Sharpe, *Mysticism*, its true nature and value, with a translation of the "Mystical Theology" of Dionysius, and of the letters to Caius and

and Dorothea (1.2, and 5), (London and Edinburgh: Sands, 1910; and St. Louis, Mo.: B. Herder, 1910), p. 95.

53. Howard Rollin Patch, *The Other World* (Cambridge, Mass.: Harvard University Press, 1950), p. 190.

54. Moorman, *loc. cit.*, pp. 78, col. 2, 79, col. 1.

55. *Ibid.*, pp. 77, col. 1; 791, col. 2.

56. *Ibid.*, p. 80, col. 2.

57. *Ibid.*, p. 81, col. 1.

CHAPTER VI

THE TRUTH CONCEALED IN A STORY

Level 2

The second level of meaning, according to the churchmen, may be illustrated by the following interpretation of Noah's drunkenness (Genesis 9.20-27), an interpretation accepted by medieval authorities, including Ambrose, Augustine, Isadore of Seville, and Rabanus Maurus:

> Noah, sinful in drunken nakedness, was none the less in that sin a type of sinless Christ, who, naked in the Crucifixion, was in the Passion as it were inebriated by the Cup of the Agony, and this, moreover, like Noah, in his own house, that is, among his own race and kindred. Even the jeering of Ham was not missing, nor the later scorn of mankind visited on those who jeered.[1]

Fantastic as this type of interpretation seems to us, it was commonly used in the Middle Ages to give value and edifying substance to all sorts of writings, including indecent and immoral tales. Even Dante, who seems to discount this type in his comment in *Convivio*, made use of it in the *Commedia*, or so some of his interpreters say.

> Since anything may be a symbol of that which is its divine exemplar, Dante's penitence for his own actual guilt is rightly a type of Christ's pleading his willing and innocent assumption of the burden of the sins of all the world. [So, also, Dante's journey through Hell is a symbol of Christ's harrowing of Hell.] If it seems strained to see in Dante, guilty of actual capitulation to *gravezza*, a type of the earthly life of Christ, let this fact be remembered; and the further fact that every character ever discussed in the Middle Ages as a type of Christ was himself

perforce guilty of sin. More than this, frequently it was in the sinful act itself that the analogy to the earthly life of Christ was found. In typology [another name for level 2] acts are viewed objectively, without primary regard to moral responsibility.[2]

The other usage, that of the poets, is the placing of a hidden meaning below the surface of the actions or events portrayed so that the wise may discover it and add it to their wisdom. Dante, in his definition of the fourfold method quoted above, illustrated the usage by a thought he found under the "fair fiction" of Ovid's remarks about Orpheus and his lyre; but he also illustrated it much more fully in his analysis of two of his own poems in the second and third sections of *Convivio*. Each of the poems on the literal level has to do with Dante's love of a lady, but on the allegorical level the lady is Philosophy and all the things said about her and the poet's feeling for her apply on the higher level to the love of wisdom.

In modern terms what Dante calls a truth hidden under the cloak of a story is what we would call the theme of a work (poem, play, short story, novel, or whatever it may be), the sum total of thought to which every word of the work contributes. It is the meaning derived when all the action, its causes, its implications, its results, are brought into focus. For purposes of teaching one may state the theme of a story briefly, as Tate and Gordon in the following lines state briefly the theme at Flaubert's "A Simple Heart":

> On the literal level it is the story of a peasant woman to whom nothing of any moment ever happened. We are convinced that Felicité is a good woman, a better woman than her mistress. Still, she dies ill, poor, and neglected. Nowadays we would be tempted to say that her life was a failure. On the allegorical level, however, she is eminently successful; the vision which she has as she is dying convinces us that she will go straight to heaven. We are not sure that anybody else in the story will.[3]

But this is not really the theme of the story: it is merely a coarse and limited approximation of the idea which is given delicate and complex expression through a multitude of details and delimiting subtleties in the story itself, and no words except those of the story can express exactly that thought. We need to remember this when we try to state the theme of a work, for the real meaning is "between the lines," i.e., in the artistry of the work. Unless a story is a poor, scrawny, undeveloped thing, not even its author can express its meaning in a few words; and whenever an author tries to do so by adding a moral or a tag at the end, he is either confessing the inadequacy of his story, or (as D. H. Lawrence said[4]) lying.

Since the allegorical interpretation of literature according to the usage of the theologians has been in ill repute since the Renaissance and a subject of scorn and merriment among readers since the eighteenth century, it is not surprising that no one has given much thought to this sort of interpretation of the *Pearl*. However, one such interpretation deserves consideration. It holds the main divisions of the *Pearl* symbolize the whole history of mankind: section 1, the narrator in the garden symbolizes mankind waiting in wretchedness for the Incarnation; sections 2-16, the appearance of the child and her teaching of the man represent the coming of Jesus and his ministry, leading up to his death (which the child describes vividly in section 14), sections 17-19, the narrator's vision of Jesus leading the procession of saints in heaven symbolizes the Resurrection; and section 20, the narrator, back in the garden, content to await God's will, symbolizes mankind waiting for Christ's Second Coming. The parallels (even the one between the child telling the Parable of the Vineyard, citing and explaining passages from the Old Testament, trying to make the narrator understand the nature of heaven, and Christ telling his parables, citing the Old Testament, and trying to make his disciples understand about heaven) are clear, and it may be that this is the meaning intended by the author.

Allegorical interpretations of the *Pearl*, in accordance with the usage of the poets, are also scarce, and this may seem surprising, for numerous American textbooks since Brooks and Warren's *Understanding Poetry* have made a staple exercise of finding the theme or meaning of stories and poems. However, many readers prefer to think of a story as "a slice of life," and I have heard such persons say after reading a story with a strong primitivistic theme (one that uncovers savage or irrational elements in a civilized person or community), "What I like about it is that it's just a good story, a slice of life, with no moral and no thought content." The Victorians, on the contrary, used to like the story with a moral – but they too shied away from intellectual insight. Comments on the moral meaning of the *Pearl*, as will be seen in the next chapter, are numerous.

The principal comments on the intellectual meaning of the *Pearl* are those by Osgood and Fletcher. Osgood says:

> ...The Pearl may be considered allegorical, somewhat as Dante's pilgrimage or *Sartor Resartus* is, in certain respects, allegorical. Under the concrete and at least partly imaginary form of the dream lies a serious, almost prosaic, experience, familiar to all men of high spiritual aspiration. In early or middle life they often seem to themselves to have achieved real wisdom, and to have laid hold upon the truth, but a sudden shift of fortune, or stroke of grief destroys both faith and creed. Then comes the bitter and violent reaction, succeeded by indifferentism; but by slow degrees the ugly visitation becomes transformed and idealized, until it is the means of entering a new life of true wisdom and peace. This is the experience figured in *The Pearl*.[5]

Fletcher points out that the child's words to the narrator "I rede þe forsake þe worlde wode,/ & porchase þy perle maskelles" imply the parable of which the poem is chiefly an allegorical interpretation:

> ...the kingdom of heaven is like unto a man that is a merchant seeking goodly pearls: and having found one pearl of great price, he went and sold all that he had, and bought it.

Fletcher continues:

> To win the Pearl is to win back innocence, the quality of the little child. Without innocence, that "pretiosa margarita," which costs all else that one has in this world, none can enter heaven.

Innocence is not only the quality which wins heaven, it is also the quality of heaven. As Christ had said: "To such is heuenrych arayed."

So...the poet's babe is not only the exemplum, of his sermon, but also example for him and all others. Only by humbling himself as this little child, by sacrifice of all else regaining his lost innocence, may he enter into the kingdom where she is. So the "pearl" takes on still another signification: it is his lost innocence as well as his lost innocent. And in this aspect, his lament is that of the contrite heart groping in the darkness for its lost hope.[6]

Perhaps this is all that can be said now about the second level of meaning in the *Pearl*, but surely more will be said in the future.

Chapter VI

Endnotes

1. H. Flancers Dunbar, *op. cit.*, p. 290.

2. *Ibid.*, pp. 289-290.

3. Caroline Gordon and Allen Tate, *op. cit.*, pp. 455-456.

4. *Studies in Classic American Literature* (New York: 1923, rptd., Garden City, N. Y.: Doubleday, 1953), p. 13.

5. *The Pearl*, ed. Osgood, pp. xxxvi-xxxvii.

6. Fletcher, "The Allegory of the Pearl," *loc. cit.*, pp. 2-3, 21.

CHAPTER VII

THAT WHICH BELONGS TO THE CENTURIES

Level 3

The third level of meaning is the moral, or tropological, and it is this that Dante found most interesting and delightful. "Morality is the beauty of philosophy," he said, "for just as the beauty of the body follows from the proper disposition of the members, so the beauty of wisdom which is the body of philosophy...follows from the disposition of the moral virtues which enable her to give pleasure perceptibly to the senses." The two branches of morality are the practical and the speculative, and in this sense "practical" means "engaged in action," and "practical employment of the mind consists in acting by our own agency virtuously, that is, uprightly, with prudence, temperance, courage, and justice." Speculative employment of the mind, on the other hand, "consists not in acting through our own agency, but in reflecting on the works of God and of Nature." The object of both forms of activity is to bring us closer to God and the state of heavenly bliss; thus they constitute "our blessedness, and our highest happiness."[1]

To the modern ear, impatient of moral platitudes, these words may seem distasteful. We are much more inclined to agree with Hemingway's Lieutenant Henry, who thought that all the high-sounding words like *honor* and *sacrifice* were empty and embarrassing. Nevertheless every writer of stories, including Hemingway, is concerned with human conduct, and every writer views it in relation to some code of values. In this sense, then, modern writers and readers are still concerned with the moral, or tropological level, thought they do not call it by that name and they probably would not agree with Dante's view or with the medieval idea that "Virtue inseparably accompanies wisdom."

Just as the narrator of the *Pearl*, on the second level, might be said to represent Man on his earthly pilgrimage, concerned with the wind and weather and physical circumstances; so, on the third level, he might be said to represent Man in the spiritual sense, concerned with right and wrong and his future destiny; and thus he has been specifically interpreted by Marie P. Hamilton, E. T. Donaldson, and John Conley. Hamilton speaks of him as "a type of whole race of fallen man, called to salvation," a man like Dante in the *Commedia*, though less learned;[2] and Donaldson says he is "mankind whose heart is set on a transitory good that has been lost–who, for very natural reasons, confuses earthly with spiritual values."[3] Conley says he is "natural man–variously termed, in the Christian tradition, homo animalis, carnalis, or sensualis."[4]

The girl in the poem, in strong contrast to the narrator, "typifies the soul made pure by sacramental grace through the merit of Christ" and thus epitomizes all souls "in like condition," Hamilton says.[5] Others have presented the same or a similar identification. "Tropologically," D. W. Robertston, Jr., concludes, she "is a symbol of the soul that attains innocence through true penance and all that such penance implies."[6] Schofield, who launched the allegorical interpretation of the *Pearl*, first insisted that she personified "Clean Maidenhood," but later (1909) added, "I confess that I am not now so much concerned to establish any particular allegorical teaching dominating the poem, as to obtain recognition of the fact that many sorts of allegorical suggestions are present in it, that the Pearl is a representative of the Brides of the Lamb, a representative, of 'the sweetness of celestial life.'" And he adds again, "...primarily an emblem of chastity."[7] Different, but related interpretations are those of Edwin Wintermute, who says that the girl represents "sanctifying grace, the possession of which is essential to the enjoyment of the Kingdom of Heaven,"[8] and Milton Stern, who suggests that she symbolizes faith.[9]

If we keep in mind the general character of the third level and the fact that the narrator stands for mankind seeking heaven, we may find a more meaningful identification of the girl than those given above. It is related to Hamilton's suggestion that the garden pictured in the *Pearl* represents the Church.[10] She points out that the garden-symbol for the Church was generally a favorite with the Church Fathers and other theological writers and was used repeatedly by Dante. Thus the Garden of Eden was often cited as a symbol of the Church; so likewise the garden of the Song of Solomon, with its curative herbs, for the Church also could be said to yield curative herbs for the wounds of sin.

If then the *erbere* for the *Pearl* represents the Church and the narrator represents sinful Man, the child of the poem is clearly an intercessor for man, and the identification proposed by Fletcher[11] becomes meaningful. From his examination of the poem he cited six types of evidence to show that the child symbolized the Virgin Mary.

First, she is crowned "in betrothal with the very words attributed to [God], when crowning Mary:

'Cum hider to me, my lemman swete,
For mote ne spot is non in þe.'" (763-764)

The words are those of the Song of Solomon, 4.7-8, a passage which is given an elaborate interpretation in *De Laudibus B. Mariae Virginis*, a monumental statement of medieval belief and doctrine by Albertus Magnus (?1206-1280).[12]

Second, she is painted "in the very colors of the symbolic portraits of Mary": "a vision of white and gold." Her whiteness is like ivory (178) and she shone "as glysnande golde" (165). So also is Mary described, and the ivory and the gold have symbolic meaning. As Albertus explains (*op cit.* X, iv, 3), "Ebur castitas,...aurum humilitas" (Ivory stands for chastity,...gold for humility). The poet also compares the child's whiteness to that of the lily:

"þy colour passeȝ þe flour-de-lys." (753)

Likewise Albertus says of Mary, "propter candorem comparatur ipsa lilio" (because of her radiant whiteness she is like the lily), *ibid.*, V, ii, 19.

Third, the child has golden hair (213), as Mary did, "signifying her golden thoughts." Vere enim cogitationes ejus fuerunt aureae." (Truly her thoughts were golden), *ibid*, V, ii, 7.

Fourth, the child is adorned with pearls (217-219), and so was the Virgin "universarum virtutum margaritis adornata" (adorned with all the virtues of the pearl), *ibid.*, IV, ix, 7.

Fifth, the child is herself a "perle" (282). So also is Mary a pearl, for she was symbolized in the pearl of the parable. "Ipsa est enim pretiosa margarita." (She is a precious pearl), II, iii, 4.

Sixth, the child is "synglere" (unique), and this word (Latin *singularis*) is "virtually consecrated" to Mary. She is "Virgo *singularis*" (XII, iv, 28), unique in beauty. Her "devotees love to ring changes on the word." Thus Albertus enumerates her unique excellences: "in *singulari* actione vel bona operatione,...in *singulari* passione vel martyrio,...in *singulari* transito vel ascensu de munde ad Deum,...in *singulari* sepultra,...in *singulari* sublimatione,...in *singulari* concessu as dexteram Filii,...in *singulari* potestate," IV, iv 3. Similarly St. Bonaventura speaks of "Maria *singulariter*, tam corpore quam anima,...O vere *singulariter* beatam domum, quae sola tam *singulariter* talem meruit habere Dominum...Iste *singularis* Mariae Dominus sic *singulariter* cum Maria fuit" – with six more repetitions of *singulariter* (*Speculum B. Mar. Virg., Lect.* x).[13]

The poem, viewed in this light, is an "extended exemplum," as Stern calls it. The theme, in Conley's words, "might be called the sovereign theme of the Christian tradition...: the nature of happiness, specifically false and true happiness." The natural man, represented by the narrator, had placed his confidence in worldly things and had found happiness in love of his "pearl." Since sin consists in preferring the temporal good to the immutable good, he was a sinner and "al that evere he hath drawen of the noble good celestial," he loses, in the words of Chaucer's commentary on Boethius' *Consolatio*. Conley classifies his sin as avarice, an "inordinate desire" for a temporal good, or, preferably, *stultitia* (folly), "the sin proper to homo animalis."[14] But these were not his only sins, for his refusal to accept God's will, his unwillingness to take consolation from either "resoun" or the "kynde of Kryst" evidence his possession of the greatest and the deadliest of sins – pride, which the angel in Paul's vision told him, "radix omnium malorum...est" (...is the root of all evil).[15] And, as St. Bernard says, "Just as pride comes from ignorance of self, so does ignorance of God beget despair."

The remedy, St. Bernard continues, is knowledge.

> The knowledge of yourself is...the first step towards the knowledge of God; He will become visible to you through His own Image which is being renewed in you, the while you are being transformed from splendour unto splendour, by beholding boldly and with open face the glory of the Lord.[16]

From these sins – desire, pride, folly, rebellion, despair, even lust and adultery – mankind is saved, not by merit, or by mankind's own effort, but by the everflowing grace of God through the intercession of Mary.

> Regnum Die consistit in duobus, scilicet in misericordia et justitiam: et Filius Dei sibi quasi retinuit justitiam velut dimidiam partem regni, matri concessit misericordiam quasi dimidiam aliam partem. Unde et dicitur regina misericordiae, et Filius sol justitiae.
>
> The reign of God is founded on two things: namely, mercy and justice. And apparently the Son of God has retained justice as his part of the reigning power and has granted to his mother the power of mercy. So she is called the Queen of Mercy and he is called the Sun of Justice.[17]

For the narrator of the *Pearl* the sky is opened, to him appears a being who possesses in supreme degree the virtues that are the opposites of his sins – love and knowledge of God, humility, wisdom, purity – and who teaches him patiently and lovingly to know both himself and God; and he is brought back to earth with the opportunity of becoming a precious pearl of Christ's.

According to Robertson, the poet's emphasis on the tropological level produced the homiletic character of the poem. Robertson adds:

> To most medieval thinkers, it is necessary for the reason to grasp a concept before the will can desire what that concept represents. This fact accounts for the elaborate doctrinal exposition in the poem. The poet wished his audience to understand the concept of innocence and that of the denarius awarded those who realize innocence. He also wished his audience to desire these things.[18]

In Hamilton's words, "the poet's design, identical with Dante's, is 'to remove those living in this life from a state of wretchedness and lead them to a state of blessedness.'"[19]

The lesson of the poem, Sister Mary V. Hillman says, is as follows: "Heaven is not to be secured by presumption or by opposition to God's will (1199-1200) but by co-operation. This co-operation is evidenced by those who reject the thraldom, the love-dominion (luf-daungere, 11) of earthly good, purchasing by renunciation of such inordinate attachment to them, that flawless pearl (743-744), eternal happiness. This teaching...belongs to the centuries – even to the twentieth."[20]

Chapter VII
Endnotes

1. *Dante's Convivio*, tr. Jackson, pp. 180, 268, 269.

2. Hamilton, PMLA 70 (September, 1955), 810.

3. Donaldson, "Chaucer the Pilgrim," PMLA 68 (September, 1954), 934.

4. Conley, JEGP 54 (September, 1955), 343.

5. Hamilton, *loc. cit.*, 806.

6. "The Pearl as a Symbol," MLN 65 (1950), 160.

7. Schofield, "Symbolism, Allegory, and Autobiography in *The Pearl*," *loc. cit.*, 638.

8. "*The Pearl's* Author as Herbalist," MLN 64 (1949), 84.

9. "An Approach to *The Pearl*" JEGP 54 (1955), 686-687.

10. Hamilton, *loc. cit.*, 814.
    Elizabeth Petroff, by contrast, argues that it is more important to see the garden as being linked allegorically to the garden of Eden and the vineyard of the Parable: "The fall in the garden means that men will continually yearn for the home from which they have been expelled and to which they may return only after death. When the narrator returns to his garden, he can see its nature with the eyes of spirit and realize its beauty as a promise of heaven, its dryness as a fact of the human condition. He knows that the water the garden lacks can be found on Earth in the sacraments of the Church. At the same time, he is able to recognize in this garden the vineyard of the Lord" (191).
    Johnson too stresses the connection between the transformation in the garden and the gardens of Christian myth: For medieval poets and exegetes, gardens had a good deal of figurative potential because of their associations with human failure, desire, and renewal" (181).

11. Fletcher, *loc. cit.*, 5, 6. Several more recent commentators have argued for a link between Mary and the *Pearl* maiden – see Elizabeth Petroff (182), for instance. Petroff points out that "an earlier English visionary, Christina of Markyate, had a vision on the Feast of the Assumption in which Mary spoke of her from Heaven, dressed in white garments and wearing a crown of white pearl" (183).
    Davenport rather fancifully argues that the Maiden might be seen as "the Dreamer's *alter ego*, combining a number of different aspects of the narrator's own nature" (37). This rather arbitary contention is not very convincingly demonstrated in the actual reading

of the text. In similar vein, Christopher Caroll in chapter 3 of his dissertation discusses "the division between the Dreamer and the Maiden and their dramatic interaction as parts of the self (will-reason, emotion-knowledge, experience-authority)" (2336A).

Johnson, who argues for an analogy between the risen Christ's meeting with Mary Magdalene and the narrator's encounter with the Pearl maiden, sees the Pearl maiden and the narrator as being analogues of Christ and Mary Magdalene respectively (cf. bibliography for citation).

12.   *Idem.*, 6-7.

13.   *Idem.*, 7-15.

14.   Conley, *loc. cit.*, 341-342, 344-345.

15.   *Sancti Bernardi Opera*, II, Sermo XXXVII, p. 12. The translation is by a Religious of C. S. M. V., *St. Bernard on the Song of Songs*: pp. 109-110.

16.   *Ibid.*, Sermo XXXVI, iv, 6 ad fin., p. 8.

17.   Albertus Magnus, De Laud. B. Mar. Virg., VI, xiii, 3, cited by Fletcher, *loc. cit.*, 13.

18.   Robertson, *loc. cit.*, 160.

19.   Hamilton, 811.

20.   Hillman, *loc. cit.*, 248.

CHAPTER VIII

ONE OF GOD'S SECRETS

The fourth level of meaning, the anagogical, is concerned with things "beyond the senses," Dante said, and it can be found through the spiritual interpretation of writing which "even in the literal sense gives intimation of higher matters." As an illustration he cited "that song of the prophet which says that, when the people of Israel went up out of Egypt, Judea was made holy and free." This, he said, is literally true, but "that which is spiritually understood is no less true, namely, that when the soul issues forth from sin she is made holy and free as mistress of herself."[1] Other medieval sources make plain that the anagogical is specially concerned with the spiritual life and that the anagogic path is "the way up from man and multiplicity to unity and God." For the mystic the way to union with God is through contemplation and inward vision. For the ordinary Christian it is through (1) "repentance and restoration to divine favor" by faith in Christ crucified and (2) rebirth in Christ, "effected by the Holy Spirit in the Church through the sacraments." Both of these ways, according to the Church Fathers, depend upon "an act of divine grace given through Christ."[2]

The *Pearl* "even in the literal sense" clearly gives "intimation of higher matters." As shown in Chapter II, it deals with the beatific vision and it demonstrates that God's sacrifice is central to heaven as it is to earth. It also says indirectly but clearly that it presents "some" of God's mysteries. The narrator, who beholds the vision of heaven and is admitted to some of God's secrets, is not a mystic, however, and he does not win his view of the heavenly mysteries through contemplative procedures – fasting, prayer, the purgation of the senses, or the painful steps upward through darkness. Instead, he is granted God's favor in the midst of his sinfulness, through the intercession of the child in heaven and the overflowing grace of Christ.

About the part played by the sacraments in the achievement of his vision, the poem does not say anything directly, but the child does speak beautifully about the source of the water of baptism and the wine of the Eucharist in the water and blood from Christ's wound and about the wonderful effects of the rites (646-660). Also, in the last stanza of the poem, abruptly and, as some would say, gratuitously, the Eucharist is mentioned again, as though the author wished to be sure that the reader kept it in mind. Nor is this all.

Near its climax the poem indirectly raises a question about the Eucharist: the child, telling of her life in heaven, says, "He [the Lamb of God] myrþe₃ vus alle at vch a mes" (862); and the reader if alert to the religious significance of the poem asks himself, is Mass celebrated in heaven? If so, how?

The poem answers the question. In its final scene (1095-1152), a great procession fills the city of God "wythouten sommoun" and at its head the Lamb moves proudly. While the aldermen fall at his feet and legions of angels scatter incense, a song of joy rings out while a spreading wound appears near the Lamb's heart and the blood pours forth.[2a]

That this scene is intended to represent the Mass is indicated by (1) the renewal of Christ's bleeding and (2) the joy and adoration of the participants. Though the Lamb is sorely hurt, his looks are "gloryous glade" and the great multitude responds with joy. The narrator looked at the Brides of the Lamb, and he saw among them the child, who had told him that the Lamb "myrþe₃ vus alle at vch a mes":

Lorde, much of mirþe wat₃ þat ho [she] made
Among her fere₃ þat wat₃ so quyt! (1149-1150)

The repetition of the word *mirþe* helps to make doubly clear that this is the Mass that the child was talking about earlier.

What connection there may be between the Mass in heaven and the Mass on earth is not immediately clear, but it is well to remember that in medieval religious poetry the most important thoughts may be hidden, as St. Jerome explained, to render them more precious, "seeing that they are won only after effort." In other words, you have to dig a little to find the truths and then you value them more.

In medieval times a great deal was written about the symbolism of the Mass. In Gulielmus Durantis *Rationale divinorum officiorum*, one of the ten books on the basis of which all medieval life can be understood, according to Male,[3] the Mass is interpreted as symbolizing the history of the world. Part I, from the Introit to the Offertory, symbolizes "the preparation of the world for the Incarnation; Part II, from the Offertory to the Agnus Dei, "the Ministry and the Passion of Christ"; Part III, from the Agnus Dei to the kiss of peace, the Resurrection; and Part IV, from the Communion to the end, "the days of waiting and the coming of the Holy Spirit."[4]

Look back now at the allegorical interpretation of the *Pearl* in Chapter VI. There you will see that the *Pearl* can also be interpreted as symbolizing the history of the world: Part I, mankind waiting in wretchedness for the Incarnation; Part II, the ministry and death of Jesus; Part III, the Resurrection; and Part IV, mankind waiting for Christ's will to be fulfilled.

This parallel between the Mass and the poem would have been sufficient to make clear to the medieval reader the doctrine of the Mass that the author of the *Pearl* intended to confirm through vision and symbolism, for it was a doctrine with a great history and once held mighty sway over the hearts of men. It originated in the early history of the Church, prior to the Council of Nicaea in 325, but first appeared merely as incomplete hints: (1) that the Eucharist is associated with the sacrifice of the Cross; (2) that the Eucharist is also associated with Christ's heavenly life.[5] In St. Clement, St. Irenaeus, and Origen, it begins to assume a more definite form:

> To Origen the centre of Christian life and worship was in the perpetual pleading of the ascended Lord at the Father's throne. In the heavens are an altar and a sacrifice, not an altar of wood or stone or a sacrifice of carnal things, but the abiding offering of that sacred Manhood which the Son of God took for the salvation of his creatures in the Incarnation, the blood of which He shed in His death. In that offering the holy dead and the priestly society of the Church on earth have their place

and share....To it there is access in Communion, and he who keeps the feast with Jesus is raised to be with Him in His heavenly work.[6]

St. Gregory the Great gives the doctrine in more complete form and conveys the ideas through pictures that still have imaginative appeal:

(The Eucharist in a mystery) renews (reparat) for us the death of the only-begotten Son, who, though He rising from the dead dieth no more and death shall not again have dominion over Him, yet living in Himself immortally and incorruptibly is again sacrificed on our behalf in this mystery of the sacred oblation...Let us think of what kind this sacrifice on our behalf is, which to set us free ever represents the passion of the only-begotten Son. For who of the faithful can hold it doubtful that in the very hour of the sacrifice at the voice of the priest the heavens are opened,...the bands of the angels are present, things lowest are brought into communion with the highest, things earthly are united with the heavenly, and the things that are seen and those that are unseen become one?[7]

In the centuries that followed, these ideas and pictures were repeatedly echoed; for example, in the Confession of the Faith, ascribed to Alcuin:

...although with bodily eyes I see the priest offering bread and wine at the altar of the Lord, yet by the gaze of faith and by the pure sight of the heart I behold the...true High Priest, the Lord Jesus Christ, offering Himself,...Verily He Himself is the priest, He Himself is the sacrifice:...Christ Himself speaks daily in His priests. He is the word which sanctifies the heavenly Sacraments...Therefore in this most holy offering of the Lord's body and blood common worship is presented to God both by the priests and by the whole family of the house of God...I do not doubt that the citizens of heaven are present at this mystery, so that by means of the ministrations and prayers of the angels, as at the altar on high, it is offered in the sight of the divine majesty. For, if in that home there is a sacrifice of perpetual praise and a perpetual priest, there is a perpetual priest and a perpetual altar in heaven,...[8]

This concept captured the imagination of the Middle Ages. At the moment of Communion men felt the presence of heaven, heard the chorus of angels, and knew that the Church in heaven and the Church on earth is one; and it was as a setting for this drama that the great cathedrals were built and men lavished their labor, their gold, and their jewels upon them and created the rich symbolism of sculpture and painting and woodcarving. In that drama, repeated daily, they found "the key of heaven; ...union with their own loved ones who were dead; ...a personal relation with the Incarnate God."[9]

Anagogically the *Pearl* presents its own dramatization of the Mass. The garden represents the cathedral or church. The man symbolizes the Church Militant; the child, the Church Triumphant. At the moment of communion the man beholds the procession of saints, sees the sacrifice of the Lamb, and hears the song of adoration and joy that strikes "þur₃ þe vrþe to helle."

It was this aspect of the poem that captivated Garrett, to the virtual exclusion of all its other meanings. He imagined the poem as arising in the poet's mind as he stood in the church and gazed at "the Elevated Host in the hands of the priest... – round, white, like a pearl, the meeting place of heaven and earth – a pearl, Margaret [margarita, the Latin word for *pearl*] – something like this would, I think, be the train of thought which would bring the germ of the poem to him. I believe," he adds, "that the poet conceives the poem as taking place within the church..., quite regardless of the convention of the arbor and the grass."

So, in his interpretation, the song that the narrator hears (19-20) represents "the chanting of the choir," the odors (46) represent the incense of the church service. The only saints mentioned in the poem are Mary and John, he says (forgetting Matthew and John the Baptist, who are each mentioned once), and the narrator would need "only to raise his eyes to the rood-beam [of the church], and he would see them standing at the foot of the Cross."

"Within the frame of a great pearl," Garrett continues, "the poet sees his lost Pearl in the presence of the Lamb of God, a very member incorporate in the mystical body of Christ; and she teaches him that through the grace of God as granted in the Eucharist it is given to him to become a member of this body, thus to be forever united with his pearl as parts of the great pearl, the mystical body of Christ."

Accordingly the poem follows the "course mapped out by the Church to be observed by one who had lost a dear one by death,...that is, to cease mourning and seek aid...in the holy Sacrifice of the Eucharist...If the soul of the departed were imperfect the Eucharist was the greatest offering that might be made for reparation and cleansing; if the soul were pure enough to enter heaven, the Eucharist was the most intimate meeting place where the lonely mourner might flee for communion with his loved one. Yet this contact must be sought through the mediation of and in the presence of Christ, in His Sacrament.

"The great danger in an exposition of the place which the Eucharist held in the spiritual life of the fourteenth century," Garrett adds, "is not exaggeration, but understatement...Nowadays it is difficult to appreciate the awe, the delight, the ecstasy with which men approached it. There the contact with Christ was as real as and more vital than was that of the Magi at Bethlehem. There they brought in the same worshipful awe all the gifts that hearts burning with love could lay at His feet. There they were lifted out of time and space and rapt into union with the eternal spring of energy. For a time individuality was merged into oneness with all perfection. It is this oneness of the whole Church at the Mass – the Church Militant, the Church Expectant, and the Church Triumphant – which...Meucci has attempted to express in his painting of the Elevation, and greatest of all, the brothers Van Eyck in the marvelous Adoration of the Lamb,..."[10]

In spite of what Garrett says above, the most dramatic phase of the concept dramatized by the *Pearl* – the oneness of the sacrifice in heaven and the sacrifice on earth – was already almost lost when the *Pearl* was being composed. The concept had never been clearly defined doctrinally, and the medieval Church had no established dogma on the point.[11] In Peter Lombard there is no reference to any connection between the Eucharist and Christ's sacrifice in heaven;[12] and in St. Thomas Aquinas the heavenly sacrifice, though referred to, is little emphasized.[13] The first heavy attack on this concept of the Mass came from Duns Scotus in the late thirteenth or early fourteenth century. With his cold logic he established that the sacrifice of the Mass is obviously not the same as the sacrifice of the Cross and is clearly of less significance; that the offering is not made by Christ himself or by the faithful in heaven, but by the priest; and that its value is not due to the priest, but to the earthly Church. Its merit, which is given it by the Church, is therefore finite.[14] From this view it is only one more step to the view of Wycliffe, who denied the authority of the Church[15] and thus reduced the value of the sacrifice of the Mass to nothing.

The *Pearl* not only confirms the sacrifice in heaven by a vivid portrayal of Christ actually making the sacrifice, but also, through its narrative, illuminates the medieval faith behind the concept. The story of the *Pearl* is built around the working of the narrator's "wreched wylle." In the beginning he refuses to accept the comfort offered by the nature of Christ (53-56) and at each successive climax, willfully and stupidly, he says or does the wrong thing. At the end, against every counsel and warning given by the child from heaven, he tries to plunge into the waters that separate him from the sainted dead and thus break into heaven by force. Since the narrator represents all mankind, his actions bring home the truth that man, so long as he lives, is never free from presumptuous folly and rebelliousness; and from this perverseness, in the medieval view, comes mankind's compelling need and the astonishing graciousness of Christ, who sacrificed himself not just once at Golgotha but does so daily, hourly, eternally through the Mass in heaven.

It may be that the narrator of the *Pearl* qualifies as a real prophet in the biblical sense. At the Council of Trent, more than two hundred years after he had his vision, the Church confirmed that Christ "offers himself daily in the Mass."[16]

Chapter VIII
Endnotes

1.   *Dante's Convivio*, tr. Jackson, pp. 73-74.

2.   *Encyclopaedia of Religion and Ethics*, ed., James Hastings (New York: Charles Scribner's Sons, 1951), V. 555.

2a.   Rosalind Field concurs with this reading of the significance of the lamb's bleeding wound (17). However, she emphasizes how "independent" this "rendering" is (14): while the Lamb is often inconographically represented as wounded in manuscripts depicting the earlier chapters of Revelations, there is a "consistent absence of wounds where the Lamb appears in triumph: on Mount Zion (chapter 14), at the Marriage Feast (chapter 19), and in the New Jerusalem (chapters 21 and 22)" (13). Field argues that "as a reminder of human suffering, the flaw in the perfection of the Lamb's pearl-like fleece is directly relevant to the main problem examined by the poem, which opens with a bereaved narrator who cannot accept death and the suffering it inflicts....The final part of his vision is an eternal city in which suffering and death are transmuted into joy" (15).
      Sandra Prior's dissertation argues that "the tension" "between private lyric experience and the apocalyptic mode" is mediated by "the Eucharist which unites personal with universal and eternal with historical in a sacramental event" (975 A). Like Prior, Sklute sees "the Eucharist which unites personal with universal and eternal with historical in a sacramental event" (975 A) as providing consolation: while "the perpetual communion, the bliss of heaven" is "not available to the living man." "the Eucharist" offers him "the bliss of heaven here on Earth" (679).

3.   *Cf*. Emile Male, *Religious Art in France XIII Century*, tr. Dora Nussey (London: J. M Dent & Sons; New York: E. P. Dutton & Co., 1913), p. xiv.

4.   *Gulielmus Durandus, Rationale Divinorum Officiorum* (LVGDVNI [Laon], 1952), Prooemevm, Liber IV, i, lvii *et passim*.

5.   Darwell Stone, *A History of the Doctrine of the Holy Eucharist*, I, 49-50.

6.   *Ibid*., I, 51-52.

7.   St. Gregory, *Dial*., iv, 53, cited by Stone, I, 195.

8.   *Conf. fid*., IV, 1, 2, 3, cited by Stone, I, 201-202.

9.   Robert Max Garrett, *The Pearl: An Interpretation*, p. 9.

10. *Ibid.*, pp. 36-37, 15-16. John Gatta, Jr. in a more recent essay argues that while "Garret's...idea of applying research in liturgical backgrounds to a critical reading" is sound, his arguments is "much too narrow in scope" concerning itself with the connection of "the pearl-symbol in isolation with but one aspect of the Eucharist liturgy, the visible moment of elevation." By contrast, Gatta suggests that "the psychic transformation of the bereaved father" mirrors the "principles" of "surrender and unstinted sacrifice" that accompany the "visible offertory" in the Mass. "Another way, the Mass might have served as an inspirational model for the poem, using the multiple penny correspondences...is through the paradigmatic symbolism and transmutation process set forth in the liturgy of the Eucharist. Eucharist transformation patterns help to illuminate the Pearl poet's literary application of transformational imagery, which accompanies transmutations from sorrow to joy, loss to gain, natural fatherly love to Christ's sacramental love, and death to life" (256).

11. *Encyclopaedia of Religion and Ethics*, ed., James Hastings (New York: Charles Scribner's Sons, 1951), V, 555.

12. Stone, *op. cit.*, I, 307.

13. *Ibid.*, I, 327.

14. Duns Scotus, *Quaest. Quodl.*, xx, cited in Stone, I, 343.

15. Stone, *op. cit.*, I, 365.

16. *Concilium Tridentinum*, edidit Societas Goerresiana, collegit edidit illustravit Stefanus Ekses (Friburgi Brisgoviae: Herder), sessio XXII 17 sep. 1562, c. ii, p. 960.

CHAPTER IX

THE EVIDENCE THAT TELLS THE NAMES

In medieval literature the names of real persons and places are often veiled. Sometimes a pseudonym is used, as Boccaccio used a pseudonym for his daughter Violante in *Olympia*. Sometimes a translation of a name is used, as Chaucer used "White" for "Blanche," and "a ryche hil" for "Richmond," in the *Book of the Duchess*. In other instances only a part of the name is given, as Dante in the *Commedia* gave only the Christian name "Beatrice" and never included the family name. In still other instances a symbol or allusion is substituted for a name, as Dante used "the green claws" to mean the Ordelaffi family and alluded to Pope Boniface VIII as "the prince of the new Pharisees." A wide variety of symbols and allusions, drawn from coats of armor, banners, badges, names of places, characters in literature, animals, actual events, personal peculiarities and characteristics, etc., were also used.

This veiling is partly the result of medieval style and habit. Writers sought to add beauty and interest to their works and to induce reader participation through a richly allusive style; and some readers no doubt gained pleasure from the intellectual exercise of identifying and compiling symbols. But there are other reasons also for the veiling. Since medieval poems were often written for private audiences – that is, for a patron and his family, court, or friends – they might treat of private matters or contain material that would give offense or cause scandal if the names of the persons involved were known. In a day when illicit love was often the subject of poetry, and when poets sometimes pursued their own wooing or helped others in their amatory pursuits by means of verse, the need for secrecy is obvious. Someone's honor or life might be in jeopardy if the wrong person saw the poem and recognized the characters.

Nevertheless the veiling in medieval poems sometimes has a curious air of duplicity. A name is veiled, but the veiling seems transparent, as, for instance, Chaucer's use of "White" for "Blanche"; or various clues are offered as though the author wanted the reader to know what he was hiding. In part, this no doubt results from the fact that the poet was writing for persons to whom he had revealed his intention or who had supplied his subject or had watched the progress of his work as he wrote it, and from whom he had no intention of hiding anything. Instead, he wanted them to read or hear and understand fully, and he accordingly supplied all the details they needed to follow him. Other factors, however, may have entered into it also.

Suppose the secret was the patron's, not the poet's, and that the poet had no particular interest in hiding the secret except to maintain his profitable relation with the patron. In that case, it if seemed to him that the future fate of his poem depended on his revealing enough to make his subject understandable to others, he might possibly provide some hints. One of the most curious instances of duplicity is Boccaccio's *Amorosa Visione*, in which he hides the story of his own love for a lady, but then gives it away in an elaborate acrostic. By reading only the first letter in each line the reader may spell out a sequence of words that constitute three complete sonnets, the first two addressed to the lady whom he loves and the last addressed to the discerning reader![1]

In spite of the hints and clues, modern scholars have not found it easy to penetrate medieval veiling or to establish positive identifications of veiled figures, sometimes because of this very duplicity. For instance, when the *Roma de la Rose* refers to "The lordis sone of Wyndesore" (l. 1250),[2] can you be sure that the reference is to one of the sons of King Henry III of England? It might be a reference to someone in Arthurian romance.

In the instances where we are sure about the identity of veiled figures, the positive identification has been made possible by either (1) a direct statement by the author in the poem itself or in a letter, commentary, or another poem, as, for instance, Boccaccio identified Olympia in a letter to a friend[3] and Chaucer identified "White" in a Prologue to the *Legend of Good Women;*[4] (2) a tradition handed down from contemporaries or near-contemporaries of the poet, as, for instance, the tradition handed down by Boccaccio that has served to identify Dante's Beatrice as Beatrice Portinari;[5] (3) a secret message from the author, such as Boccaccio provided in the acrostic mentioned above; and (4) a factual context provided by the author, as, for instance, by Dante in the *Inferno* (xxvii. 37-45), when he speaks of the rulers of the Romagna in 1300 and specifically cites the "green claws" as lords of the city that bore a long siege by the French, thus making clear that he is talking about the Ordelaffi family, whose coat of arms included the claws. Once a positive identification has been made, other details spring to life and show, in relation to the identification, additional meaning. Thus, in the canto just cited, once the unnamed speaker is identified as Guido de Montefeltro, his words have added poignancy in relation to the known facts of his life.

With regard to the *Pearl*, we do not even know the name of the author, and do not have any explanation or tradition on record to help in the identification of its characters. All we have is the text of the poem, the manuscript that contains it, and the illustrations accompanying it. Nevertheless various conjectures have been made about the author and the characters. Guest proposed and Madden (1839) accepted "Huchoun of the Awle Ryale" (a Scottish poet named by Winton in his Chronicle) as the author and narrator; and Gollancz (1891) suggested Ralph Strode, described in the Memorials of Merton College as "nobilis poeta."[6] Both suggestions, however, were dropped when linguistic studies demonstrated that the poem is "in a different dialect from that which must have been spoken by either of the two men."

Another suggestion is that of C. O. Chapman (1932),[7] who nominated John de Erghome, Augustinian Friar of York in the fourteenth century, because Erghome's library is known to have contained certain books familiar to the author of the *Pearl* and because Erghome in his "Prophecy of John of Bridlington" used the same Bible stories to illustrate the same sins that "the Pearl-poet" (i.e., the hypothetical individual who wrote all four poems in MS.

Cotton Nero A x) used in *Patience* and *Cleanness*. This reasoning, however, does not seem convincing.

Other conjectures concerning the poet consist mainly of inferences drawn from the content of the *Pearl* (and the other three poems in the manuscript) with regard to his calling, his social background, and his education and training. It has been held that he was a retainer of some nobleman (Gollancz) or an ecclesiastic (Brown, Coulton), familiar with the life of a feudal castle (Osgood) and the usages of courtly life (Greene), that he received training in music in a choristers' school attached to a church, cathedral, or monastery (Chapman),[8] and that he had a special knowledge of herbs, thus suggesting the possibility of experience in an infirmary and membership in an order of canons of friars (Wintermute).[9]

Speculation regarding the identity of the girl has been more limited. Gollancz suggested that her name was "Marjory" or "Marguerite" (meaning "pearl"), and Cargill and Schlauch (1928) produced an elaborate theory to the effect that she was Margaret, daughter of the Earl of Pembroke and grand-daughter of King Edward III, a child who may have died at the age of two, and that the poem was written by "someone closely connected with her father and the court and (possibly as guardian) with the little girl herself." This identification, the authors add, "would explain the unfilal [stet], unpaternal language, the epithets (such as *ryal*) used in descriptions, and, since the earldom of the girl's father was Pembroke, the use of a western dialect by the poet, who, even though born in Wales, might well have employed West Midland English." The authors go on to suggest that the poem may have been written by one of the Earl of Pembroke's followers and suggest, for the honor, two of his clerks: John Donne and John Pratt. They hope other investigators will carry the search further and make positive demonstration. Nothing further, however, has come of this proposal.[10]

Since we lack any direct statement by the author and any contemporary tradition, our best chance to identify the characters lies in the study of whatever context the poem itself supplies. In the past, as shown by Cargill and Schlauch's attempt to identify the girl, the known or supposed facts have not furnished a sufficient basis; but it now appears that the conclusions reached in Chapter V may offer the means of establishing an identification. The conclusions there reached, with reference to the girl, were: (3) that she was connected in some way with royalty; (4) that she was placed in a convent before she was two, died before she was seven, and made some kind of commitment to the life of a nun before her death; and (5) that she was an illegitimate child, the unacknowledged daughter of the narrator. It was further concluded that she was buried, not in a graveyard, but in a garden; and that she lay in an unmarked grave.

A person fitting most of these conditions was mentioned in Chapter V. She is Eleana, or Alienor, born May 6, 1306, who was the daughter of Queen Margaret of England and putative daughter of King Edward I, was placed in the convent of Amesbury before she was two years old, died in 1311 before her fifth birthday, and was buried "with little ceremony and without a stone" to mark her grave in an unknown spot, not in a cemetery, but within the grounds of Beaulieu Abbey, Hampshire.[11]

With regard to one part of condition (4), personal commitment to the life of a nun, though we have no facts, there is no real difficulty, for it is possible that Eleana might have been allowed by the authorities at Amesbury to make that commitment before her fifth birthday because of her illness, or she might have made the vow privately without their permission or approval.

But with regard to condition (5), illegitimacy, it seems difficult to imagine she could qualify. However, certain hints in historical documents and certain facts in her background suggest the possibility that she might be illegitimate. First, a contemporary chronicle, written by the monks of Westminster, who had access to court gossip, pointedly omits the name of the child's father in its notice of her birth, saying "...domina Margareta regina Angliae Wintoniam peperit filian (the lady Margaret, queen of England, at Winchester bore a daughter)...," instead of employing the usual formula *natus est regi filius* (a child was born to the king).[12] Second, there was a wide difference in age between the King and Queen – when they married, he was sixty, and she was sixteen or seventeen – and a scurrilous comment in another chronicle ridicules the idea that he was the father of her children.[13] Third, less than a year after the death of the king, about the time when Eleana was placed in the convent at Amesbury, the new king (Edward II, the Queen's stepson, a man about her age) seized the two castles, Marlborough and

Devizes, that were part of her dower, and placed one of his chief counsellors, the stern elder Despenser,[14] in charge. This order meant that the Queen was deprived of control over her income and servants and probably was herself put under restraint. Fourth, the placing of the infant princess, not yet two years old, in a convent, away from the care of her mother, is a very unusual event and suggests that unusual circumstances prompted the action. Lastly, the burial of the child, not with King Edward's other children who had died young and were given splendid funerals and tombs, but instead, alone, without a monument or marker for her grave, in the grounds of a monastery, bears out the likelihood that she was purposely pushed out of the royal family.

If the child was illegitimate, the reason for Edward II's action is not hard to understand. To him, it no doubt seemed intolerable that a bastard – defined in English law, even if the parent were known, as the child of nobody (*filius nullius*), a person who could not be heir to anyone and who had no ancestor from whom any inheritable blood could be derived[15] – should hold a place among the royalty of England and should pass such a heritage on to her offspring. The simplest way to remedy that intolerable condition was to place the child permanently in a convent where she could never marry and, if the child's mother would not agree voluntarily, to force her to, by threat of shame, loss of dower, and imprisonment. This would be the best way to prevent a public scandal, for it would avoid any open admission of the facts and would prevent any reflection on the memory of Edward I.

The publication later in the same year of a volume in praise of Edward I was perhaps a part of the same plan, for it contains an overstrained account of the Queen's great love for her dead husband. "*Ha! bone Jesu*," she is represented as saying in Latin, "quis mihi tribuat, ut pro te moriar, domine mi rex? Mors in voto mihi est, et vita in taedio."[16] (Ha! good Jesus, who will grant me leave to die for you, my lord King? Death is my prayer, and life is weariness.)

One of the ironies involved is that the man who prepared this book was John of London, a monk at Westminster, where the chronicle was written that omits the name of the child's father.[17]

That the new King's will prevailed is shown by the fact that the child remained in the convent and the Queen's castles were restored to her later in the year. Thereafter the Queen is said to have lived quietly, devoting her time to charities.[18]

The name of the child, Eleana, may seem to run counter to what the poet implies, for she is repeatedly referred to as the narrator's pearl and is twice addressed as "perle" (241, 745); and "perle" suggests Margareta (from the Latin word for pearl), her mother's name. However, in medieval times, members of the royal family, lacking a family name "long after surnames had become universal outside the blood royal," were customarily described "by their Christian names in conjunction with a title or personal epithet, such as John 'Lackland,' or Edmund 'Crouchback'; or with a territorial appellation..., as John 'of Gaunt'"[19]; and there is a notation in one of the chronicles that Eleana was called Margareta,[20] this name being added presumably like Lackland or Crouchback in the examples above, so that the full name of the child would be Eleana Margareta.

All things considered, this evidence gives support to the conclusion that the little rejected princess, Eleana Margareta, is the child portrayed in the *Pearl*. If so, it is easy to understand why the relationship of the man and the child is never stated and why the man's identity is concealed so carefully. According to English law at that time, violation of the wife of the King, with or without her consent, was high treason and was punishable by torture, mutilation, dismemberment, and death.[21] A similar law in France was actually put into effect by Queen Margareta's brother, King Phillip the Fair, when two of his daughters-in-law were discovered in adultery. He had their lovers castrated, then actually flayed, and finally beheaded. The princesses he ordered to be imprisoned, but one of them was strangled by order of her husband.[22]

Since the poem offers no clue to the identity of the man beyond the implication that he is of the highest rank, a prince, we will turn now to another available source of information, the manuscript containing the poem. A close examination provides two aids. In the first illustration, which shows the child's grave, the man is pictured wearing a gown of red with white wrist-bands and a blue chaperon or hood.[23] As mentioned earlier, the illustrations are not only crude but inaccurate, and give no indication that the artist had read the poem with care; and the costume in the illustration is not based on any details supplied by the poem. Nevertheless it conveys interesting information. The red and white of the gown were the livery colors of the King of England, and the blue hood signified the house of Lancaster.[24] These colors would have been recognized by any Englishman of the fourteenth and early fifteenth centuries, for the red and white of the King and the blue and white of Lancaster were worn wherever the retainers and servants of the King and the Earldom or Duchy of Lancaster went about their business or pleasure.

The combining of the colors, however, was unusual, for the King's men wore only the red and white and the retainers of Lancaster only the blue and white; and the combination of colors would have been appropriate only after John of Gaunt, son of King Edward III, married Blanche, the heiress of Lancaster, and then probably only for himself and members of his family. At any rate the combination became associated with the Lancastrian kings of England, the line that began with John and Blanche's son, Henry IV, who was crowned in 1399 and was followed on the throne by his son, Henry V, and his grandson, Henry VI.

In one of the medieval paintings of Henry VI, the last king of the Lancastrian line, he is shown wearing a red gown with white wristbands, similar to that worn by the man in the illustration accompanying the *Pearl*, and, in place of the blue hood, which was worn outdoors, a blue mantle.[25] It therefore seems likely that the colors used in the illustration of the *Pearl* convey the artist's knowledge that the man who had the vision of heaven was a nobleman of the house of Lancaster.

It may seem surprising that the illustration is so revealing while the poem is so secretive. The passage of time, however, may be the key. The poem implies an illicit romance that began prior to August, 1305, resulting in the birth of Eleana Margareta on May 6, 1306, and it tells of a vision that came to the man in August, 1311, several months after the child's death, or in some subsequent August. The poem itself was written after 1350 ("the details of costume belong to the second half of the fourteenth century"[26]) and probably before 1375. When it was being written, the Queen had been dead

The narrator lying on his child's grave
(from MS Cotton Nero A x, folio 37)

The couplet that carries a secret message
(from MS Cotton Nero A 6, folio 125)

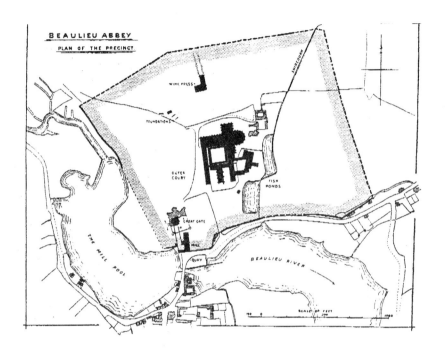

The plan of the precinct of Beaulieu
(from *A History of Beaulieu Abbey*, plate xxv)

a long while (she died young in 1318[27]) and the man who had had the vision was dead too, but people who had known him and the Queen were still living, including children and grandchildren of the Queen and children and grandchildren of his. On the other hand, in 1400 or slightly later, when the manuscript was being copied, the events were almost a hundred years in the past and no one alive would be greatly concerned about hushing up the scandal. That the artist or scribe knew the identity of the man was probably due to annotations in the manuscript from which he copied or to information furnished by descendants or other kinsmen of the man.

If we wish to seek the man in the *Pearl* among the noblemen of the house of Lancaster in 1305, the possibilities are Thomas, Henry, and John, the three sons of Edmund Crouchback, 1st Earl of Lancaster, and his wife, Blanche, the former Queen of Navarre.[28] By descent from Henry III, their grandfather, each was a prince of the blood royal. Little is known of John beyond his name, but the others were important figures: Thomas, Earl of Lancaster, having succeeded his father in 1296, and Henry, Lord of Monmouth, Kidwelly, and Carwathlan, having inherited all that his father had held on the Welsh side of the Severn.[29] Both were in their twenties and both were married. They were nephews of King Edward I, then in his sixty-seventh year, and his wife, Queen Margareta, who was younger than either of them.

The second aid is provided by a couplet on folio 125 of the manuscript. It is at the top of the page, above an illustration that shows a secret meeting between Sir Gawain and the wife of the Green Knight, but it has no demonstrable connection with the illustration, and its position in relation to the picture, as W. W. Greg pointed out,[30] shows that it was written on the page before the drawing was sketched in. The couplet reads as follows:

> My minde is mukul on on þat wil me noȝt amende
> Sum time was trewe as ston & fro schame couþe hir defende.
> (My mind is much on one that will not amend for me
> Formerly was true as stone and from shame could defend herself.)

Remembering that medieval writers sometimes left secret messages, as Boccaccio did in *Amorosa Visione*, and that various forms of secret writing were used, such as the acrostic used by Boccaccio, the present writer applied various tests to the above lines in an effort to find out whether or not they had any hidden meaning, and thus discovered that some parts of the couplet, when read backwards, seemed to contain distinguishable words. In particular, in the middle of the second line, the words "ahcs or f& [fand] not" stood out. I therefore continued to work with the couplet, hoping to find the correct way to space the letters to make words and to determine what contractions or abbreviations were used.

As I worked, I found more distinguishable words, but could not find a way to make the whole of the two lines decipherable. I finally decided that the couplet, having probably been copied into the existing manuscript from an earlier manuscript, might not have been accurately copied letter for letter, as it would have to be if the original message were to be read backwards, and that the same sort of spelling errors and substitutions that often occur in medieval manuscripts might occur also in this couplet. I therefore began to try out various substitutions in spelling, for instance, *my* for *mi*; *mynde, mynd*, and *mind* for *minde*; *micel, mukel*, etc. for *mukul*; and other common variants that might have occurred in fourteenth-century Midland English. Finally, by making six substitutions – *mukel* for *mukul, wol* for *wil, not* for *no3t, sume* for *sum, trew* for *trewe*, and *hire* for *hir* – I put the lines into the following form:

> Mi minde is mukel on on þat wol me not amende
> Sume time was trew as ston & fro schame couþe hire defende.

Read backward, going from the end of the first line to the beginning and then from the end of the second line to the beginning of the second, with þ and & treated as units, and punctuation and capitals added, the lines read as follows:

> Ed ne Mat on E.M. lowt.   Aþ? No.   Nole kum S.I.E.,
>   d. nim 'im,
> Ed nefe der, i., he þ.   uoc E.M.   Ahcs or f& not.
>   Ssaw er [ON. *eir*] t saw E.M., item us.

Some of the letters above are common medieval contractions or abbreviations: for example, in the second line, *i.* means *id est* (that is), just as *i.e.* does today; þ means *þat* (that); *t* means *et* (and).[31] Three of the other contractions, though not common, are self-explanatory and can probably be found elsewhere in medieval manuscripts: *S. I. E.* for *Seynt Iohannis Eve* (St. John's Eve); *d.* for *deuel* (devil); and *f&* for *fand*. One, *'im* for *him*, is a colloquial contraction. The other contractions seem to represent names: *Ed*, *Mat*, and the initials *E. M.*

The message may be paraphrased as follows:

> Do not yield to Ed or Mat in regard to E. M. Oath? No. He
>   will not come St. John's Eve, devil take him,
> Dear cousin Ed, that is, he who woke E. M.
>   Do not ask or inquire. Show honor and save E. M., also
>   us.

In the first line "Oath? No" is not clear; perhaps it means, "If they offer you their sworn promise, do not accept it or believe them" or it might mean, "If they ask you for your sworn promise, do not give it." In the second line *uoc* apparently means "woke spiritually" (i.e., woke the two-year-old child to be calling as a nun).[32]

The message is clear, but surprising. It does not bear directly on the poem or its content, but it seems obviously to concern Eleana Margareta, the child in the poem. At least the initials E. M. appear three times, and the content is appropriate to the period after the child was placed in the convent and while pressure was being put on the queen to force her to accept the arrangement (the king seized control of her servants and castles on March 12[33]). At this time her lover, the father of Eleana Margareta, unable to communicate directly with her, might prepare such a message and find some way to get it to her without anyone suspecting that it was a message.

The substance of the message fits the occasion: he warns her not to yield to "Ed" (i.e., the king, Edward II): he pleads with her to save "E. M." (Eleana Margareta); and he adds a plea for "us" (himself and the queen, their future happiness being tied up with the child's).

The message contains three bits of information: (1) "Ed" (the king) will not come St. John's Eve; (2) "Ed" is the sender's cousin or nephew (*nefe* was used in both senses); (3) "Ed" has an ally named "Mat."

Taking these in order, the first might mean that the queen had placed some hope of reaching a settlement of her difficulties on the outcome of a meeting with the king on St. John's Eve (June 23), and the sender warns her that the king does not intend to keep the engagement. Of course it might mean something else. Also, even if the interpretation is correct, there is no way to check up on the facts. However, the writer did check to see where King Edward was on June 23, 1308; and he found that the king was in Bristol, but that he had been at Queen Margareta's castle of Marlborough from June 19 to June 22.[34]

So they probably had their conference. If so, it did not alter Eleana Margareta's situation; she had already been at Amesbury more than two months and she remained there till her death in 1311.

The second bit of information (Ed, the king, is a nephew or cousin of the writer) ties in with the information given by the livery colors in the illustration: Thomas, Henry, and John were first cousins of King Edward II.

The third bit of information (Ed has an ally named Mat) supplies the key identification. Matilda de Chaworth was the wife of Henry,[35] and Mat is a colloquial form of her name. Thus the message reveals that Henry was the man involved.

It further reveals that Matilda had joined with the king against the queen and Eleana Margareta, no doubt for the purpose of protecting her marriage and children, including Henry's son, the future Duke of Lancaster, then eight years old. And this gives additional point and meaning to the fact that Despenser was the man appointed by the king to control the queen's castles and household. He was Matilda's stepfather.[36]

One other source of information has been discovered. At Beaulieu Abbey there is a large worn slab of marble which, it is believed, covered the grave of the Princess Eleana Margareta for centuries. In 1963, when the writer was at Beaulieu, it was not available for inspection, but he was told that it was below the floor covering in the museum in what was once the lay brothers' dining hall.

Fortunately it is carefully described in an unsigned, undated document that belonged to the second Baron Montagu of Beaulieu and was printed in Sir James K. Fowler's *History of Beaulieu Abbey* (1911), pp. 197-198. According to this description, the marble is "curiously inlaid with a white composition which is cemented into the hollows or grouves with pitch, which shews a black line all around. The white compos was afterwards engraved and the lines filled with a black composition which is for the most part effaced by being continually walked over. The representation is, as I conjecture, the figure of a lady, her head resting on a pillar standing on a bracket or Gothic pedestal under a Gothic ogee arch, adorned with ogee 5 foil on two slender pillars, terminated with pinnacles and crockets and a large finial, which supports a ducal corronet between two shields, the corronet and shields seem to have been inlaid with brass, but they are tore away, the whole is enclosed with the inscription, each letter on a separate little square of white inlaid aforesaid, of which only this is visible, of which any meaning can be made -

JESU CRIST　　: OMNIPOTENT FI, ...INTEM."

The use of a ducal coronet shows that the monument belongs to a period at least a half century later than Eleana Margareta's death, for the title of duke was not in use in England until Edward III's reign, and the ducal coronet was not used until 1362, when John of Gaunt, who had married Blanche, Henry's granddaughter, succeeded to the title of Duke of Lancaster.[37]

Most important, since the ducal coronet has no demonstrable connection with Eleana's descent from Queen Margareta or her supposed descent from King Edward I, it constitutes a recognition of the child's link with the house of Lancaster through her father and thus confirms the evidence supplied by the picture in the manuscript and the secret message.

Furthermore, as soon as the identities of the man and child are established, various details in the poem acquire additional meaning and become corroborative evidence.

Thus line 1178 implies the name of Beaulieu as the setting, using "fayre regioun" as a translation of Old French *biau lieu*.

And line 107 suggests the name of the stream that flows through the precinct of Beaulieu Abbey by referring to it as "a water...þat *schere₃*" (i.e., runs bright and clear; derived from the adjective *schere*. See O. E. D.). The actual name of the stream, given in the charter that created the Abbey in 1204, and still used today, is Shireburn[38] (Schirebourne, derived from the adjective *schere* plus *borne*, meaning a bright, clear little stream).

The narrator says that the stream runs *dry₃ly* (defined by Gordon as continually); and Shireburn, according to Fowler's *History*, had never, in the memory of the oldest inhabitant, failed to provide a constant supply of water to Beaulieu.[39]

The narrator also says,

I hoped þe water were a deuyse
Bytwene myrþe₃ by mere₃ made...,

which Gordon translates "I thought the stream was a division made by pools, separating the delights" and adds that a "general conception of the landscape and its stream flowing from pool to pool was probably suggested by the garden of Deduit in the *Roman de la Rose*."[40] But look at the map of the precinct of Beaulieu Abbey (reproduced here from Fowler's *History*, p. 62), and you will see that Shireburn in the fourteenth century flowed first into one fish pond and then into another, thus supplying the picture given by the poet.

In the confirmation charter of Edward III about 1338 mention is made of "the spring-head of the waters of Shireburn, that extends as far as the aforesaid Abbey of King's Beaulieu,"[41] and it is to this point that the child in the *Pearl* directed the narrator so that he might see his vision of heaven:

'Bow vp towarde þys borne₃ heued,
And I anende₃ þe on þis syde
Schal sve, tyl þou to a hil be vewed.' (974-976)

As noted above, the narrator twice addresses the child as *perle*, using that word to suggest her acquired name Margareta; but he also twice uses another symbol to suggest her first name Eleana (from Greek *Helenë*, meaning torch). In line 755 he addresses her as "bry₃t" and in line 769 as "maskelle₃ bryd þat bry₃t con flambe."

A number of other passages also acquire additional meaning. In line 71, when the child speaks of her death as the time "when I wente fro your worlde wete" (761), this may be an allusion to "the contrast between the rough and rainy climate of this world and the eternally bright and serene atmosphere of Heaven," as Gordon says (p. 73), but it is also a reference to the actual cycle of bad weather that began in 1308, the year Eleana Margareta was put in the convent, and continued until 1322. Hard winters, cold stormy summers, wet harvests, and incessant rain produced first dearth and eventually famine.[42]

Likewise, when the narrator says of the child that she was "nerre þen aunte or nece" (233), he is saying not only that she was nearer in blood-relationship than aunt or cousin – that is, actually his daughter – but also nearer than she was supposed to be, i.e., his first cousin, the daughter of his aunt by marriage.

Again, when he compares the child to the fleur-de-lys (195), the symbol calls to mind not only the lily as symbol of the Virgin Mary but also the lilies of France (the symbol of the French royal family) and, still more specifically, the lily as symbol of Queen Margaret, who used it on her great seal. And when the child tells the man that as a result of her death he lost but "a rose þat flowred and fayled" (269-270), the symbol may also imply her admission that she is his child – a rose of Lancaster. She never refers to herself as a lily, though the man makes the comparison twice.

The identification of the character sets the story of the *Pearl* in an historic context. Margareta was married to Edward I in 1299 as part of a treaty between France and England, fostered by Pope Boniface VIII, Dante's enemy;[43] and the resulting peace not only postponed the Hundred Years War for forty years, but also left Edward free to continue his effort to conquer Scotland, and Philip the Fair, Margareta's half-brother, free to pursue his life-long aim to destroy papal power in France.

In 1306, the year Eleana Margareta was born, Scotland rose for a third time against Edward, and the next year, while preparing to lead an army into Scotland, Edward died near the border, leaving instructions he was not to be buried till Scotland was conquered.[44] Nevertheless his son Edward II abandoned the war.

Late in January 1308 Henry of Lancaster and Queen Margareta accompanied Edward II to France for his marriage to Isabelle, daughter of Philip the Fair. (Henry was the bride's half-uncle; Margareta, her half-aunt). The king, his bride, and the rest of the party returned to England on February 7 and rested at Eltham from the fifteenth to the twentieth. Then they proceeded to London, where Edward's coronation was celebrated on the twenty-fifth, Henry carrying the rod with the dove in the ceremony.[45]

At this time perhaps the relationship of Margareta and Henry became evident to the king; or perhaps it was already a troublesome matter in his eyes. Perhaps the two were living together more or less openly. At any rate, about two weeks later, the king seized Margareta's castles, thus applying to her the provisions of a statute that "expressly punished with loss of dower the woman who eloped and abode with her adulterer."[46] He also assumed custody of their child. (The *Pearl* says that Henry and Eleana Margareta were "towen and twayned," i.e., torn apart.)

That same year hostility between the king and the house of Lancaster flared. Henry's brother Thomas, the second Earl of Lancaster, took the lead in forcing the banishment of Piers Gaveston, Edward's favorite. Four years later, after Gaveston had been recalled, banished again, and returned again, Thomas and his friends took up arms and executed the favorite.

Edward II proved to be an incompetent and unpopular king, chiefly interested in sports and frivolities and reputed to be a homosexual; but with the counsel and aid of Despenser, the same man who acted for the king in seizing Margareta's castles, he regained some of his power and in 1322 defeated Thomas and had him beheaded.[47]

In these disorders Henry took no active part. But in 1326, when Queen Isabelle and her oldest son, after a prolonged stay in France, arrived in England, proclaiming she had come to avenge Thomas of Lancaster, Henry joined her with his liege men (Chaucer's grandfather being among them[48]), and they drove the king into Wales, where he took refuge with Despenser's son, and there captured him.

Henry presided at the trial that condemned the elder Despenser to death, and for a while he acted as jailer of the king. But the queen and her paramour Roger Mortimer felt they could not be safe while the king lived, and so they took him away from Henry and put him under jailers who first tried to cause his death by ignominious treatment and poor food, but, failing in that, they murdered him, without leaving a mark on his body, by thrusting a red-hot rod through a drenching-horn into his bowels.[49]

Henry was named by Parliament as guardian of the fifteen-year-old king, Edward III, but the country was governed by Isabelle and Mortimer. When Henry was denied access to the young king, he formed a confederacy of discontented nobles and bishops; but Mortimer sent an army against him, and he did not have sufficient forces to oppose them. Since he was then counted as the foremost man in England, public opinion and the Archbishop of Canterbury interceded for him, and peace was restored.

At this time Henry's sight was failing, but he attended the Parliament held at Nottingham in October 1329, brought the young king to a realization that he had to get rid of Mortimer, and helped to plan a coup d'etat. A party entered Nottingham Castle at night by a secret passageway and seized Mortimer, who was tried and executed.[50]

Thus Edward III began his spectacular reign of fifty years. His invasion of France in 1339 marked the beginning of the Hundred Years War.

Henry became blind, devoted himself to religious activities, and built a hospital at Leicester in honor of the Annunciation. He died in 1345.[51]

The identification of the characters also gives the *Pearl* a local habitation: namely, Beaulieu Abbey, a monastery for over three hundred years, suppressed in 1538 by Henry VIII, and its buildings and land sold to Thomas Wriothesley, later 1st Earl of Southampton, whose descendants (including the 3rd earl, Shakespeare's friend and patron) have held it ever since – a place still possessing features described in the *Pearl*. Fowler, writing in 1911, pictures it vividly. "The manor," he writes, "lies in a ring-fence, of which the boundaries are formed by the [New] Forest [established by William the Conqueror in 1079], the Solent, and the Beaulieu River."

> It is beautiful at high tide, and, as some think, hardly less so when the tide is low, and its banks are covered with brown seaweed and green sea grass near the narrow stream. The river is navigable and navigated up to the quay opposite the outer gate of the abbey, and the top of the mast with the brown sail of a sea-going barge can often be seen, phantom-like, over the trees, before the boat itself comes into view.
>
> Perhaps, however, it is most beautiful at night when the sky is clear, the tide high and the moon at the full and immediately over the river, then viewed from the hill above, by Harford Wood, it looks like a dazzling stream of molten silver.[52]

"From the hill above, by Harford Wood" – that is the point from which Henry of Lancaster in his vision looked into the City of God and saw his "lyttel quene" among her "fere₃."

When he went there in August 1311 or 1312, men were cutting grain with "croke₃ kene" nearby and flowers were bright in the garden and on the mound of the child's grave – clove-scented pinks, blue gromwell, red peonies, and yellow tansy – and the great Abbey church towered in the quiet, bright air.[52a]

The church is gone – destroyed in the 1500's. And if you go there now, as the writer did in 1963, you will find the grounds crowded and noisy with tourists who have come to see Palace House (once the Great Gatehouse of the Abbey, now with alterations and additions the ancestral home of Lord Montagu of Beaulieu), the other restored buildings, the ruins, and the Montagu Motor Museum. With the noise and crowd it is hard to get the feel of a fourteenth-century Cistercian monastery; but come back at night, when the crowds are gone, and moonlight and silence touch everything, and you may find it almost as beautiful and magical as it seems in the *Pearl* and in Fowler's description.

The identification and the other material presented in this book give the *Pearl* a clear and definite identity, so that it can no longer be treated as a free scholarly preserve, open to any sort of interpretation consistent with medieval analogues or formulas.

The author is not a primitive genius from the childhood of the race. He is a man well acquainted with the learning of his day and a master of medieval veiled verse, subtle, complex, intricately beautiful.

The child is not an unknown poet's two-year-old daughter who appears in his absurd vision as a grown woman. She is a real little girl of five, born to be a princess of England, rejected for no fault of her own, destroyed by sickness in childhood, but raised in heaven to be a greater queen than any on earth.

The narrator is not a simple, private person. He is a strong, complex man facing large responsibilities, tormented by very real failings: gross ingratitude to his benefactor, the old king; adultery of a kind specifically cursed by God; the degradation of his own child, left unacknowledged and vulnerable. Did not the Bible say, "If a man lies with his uncle's wife..., they shall bear their sin; they shall die childless: and "A bastard shall not sit in the congregation of the Lord." No wonder he thought his *perle* "done out of days" and stripped of any chance of honor here or hereafter.

The presence of the secret message in the MS shows that the story of the *Pearl* was drawn from an actual account of Henry's experience which included the couplet – an account either written by Henry, who alone could supply the details, or taken down from his lips. Such an account would most likely have been written as a confession to clear the conscience of a man nearing death, and it would most surely be carefully put away, to be seen only by his heir or heirs after his death. Henry, son of the above, also wrote a confession of this kind (acknowledging his sins of the flesh, but not being too specific about them) before his death in 1361. It is a curious and interesting document, giving the name of the author written backwards as follows: ERTSACNAL ED CUD IRNEH.[53]

In all probability the *Pearl* was commissioned by Henry's son as a commemoration of his father's religious experience, first, for the private edification of his family and, perhaps, later, when those who might resent or be hurt by identification of the characters were no longer alive, for release to others who might find inspiration in its content. Poems were often thus commissioned in the Middle Ages. For instance, *Melusine* was written for the sister of the Duc de Berri, and its subject matter was compiled from records in the castle of Lusignan and from chronicles obtained from the Earl of Salisbury.[54] A metrical version of the same story was later commissioned by William, Duke of Parthenay.[55] Similarly Hartman von Aue's finest story was drawn from documents in the archives of his feudal lord.[56]

It is possible, of course, that the Duchess Blanche, rather than her father, commissioned the *Pearl*. The fact that the monument at Beaulieu bears a ducal coronet indicates clearly that she was the one who reached out to welcome into the family a little girl who had lain a long time in an unmarked grave.

Chapter IX
Endnotes

1. Giovanni Boccaccio, *Le Rime/ L'Amorosa Visione/ La Caccia de Diana*, a cure de Vittore Branca (Bari: Guis, Laterza & Figli, 1935), pp. 119-121.

2. *The Poetical Works of Chaucer*, ed. Robinson, p. 676.

3. "Epistola ad Fratrem Martinum de Signa," from *Le Lettere edite & inedite di Messer Giovanni Boccaccio*, ed. Corrazzi, quoted in *Pearl* (1921), ed. Gollancz, pp. 254-257.

4. *Chaucer*, ed. Robinson, p. 579.

5. *Tutte le Opere di Giovanni Boccaccio*, a cura di Vittore Branca (Milano: Arnoldo Mondadori, 1965) VI, "Exposizioni sopra la Comedia di Dante," a cura di G. Padoan, 114.

6. Madden, *Syr Gawayne*, p. 302; *Pearl* (1921), ed. Gollancz, p. xlvii-xlix.

7. "The Authorship of the *Pearl*," PMLA 47 (1932), 350.

8. *Pearl*, (1921), p. xlii; Brown, PMLA 19 (1904), 126; Coulton, MLR2 (1906), 39; Osgood, p. liii; Greene, PMLA 40 (1925), 827; Coolidge Otis Chapman, "The Musical Training of the *Pearl* Poet," PMLA 46 (1931), 180.

9. Wintermute, MLN 64 (1949), pp. 83-84. Eldredge summarizes some of the other claims made for the poet's identity: "Edwin Wintermute arguing solely from the single mention of *gromlyoun* in line 43 proposes that the poet must have been an apothecary or at least must have worked in an infirmary....Ormerod Greenwood proposes one Hugh Mascy as author of the four poems" (Eldredge, 191-192).

    Clifford Peterson argues that there is anagramatic textual evidence linking the author of the *Pearl* poem to the author of *St. Erkenwald* – an author with a name like Massey (53).

10. PMLA 43 (1928), pp. 108, 118, 122.

11. Francis Lancelot, *op. cit.*, I, 164. The name Eleana is given in an Issue Roll (Mich., 4 Ed. II, August 28 and November 20), cited by Sir James Fowler, *A History of Beaulieu Abbey A. D. 1204-1539*, ed. Henry Richards Luard (Rolls Series, 1890), III, 130. record the birth of a princess, but the usual formula for the birth of a prince is "natus est regi filius [a son was born to the king]. In the birth notices of Queen Margareta's two sons, the name of the father was also omitted.

12. *Flores Historian*, ed. Henry Richards Luard (Rolls Series, 1890) III, 130, cf. III, 61, 13, 32, note 8. The section beginning with events of 1266 and concluding with those of 1326 was written by various monks at Westminster. See Luard's introduction, I, xliii; also *The Collected Papers of Thomas Frederick Tout* (Manchester, 1934), II, 289-301.

13. "[Cum Rex] autem illam in societatem tori recepisset, statim ab [illo] impraegnata est." "Annales Angliae et Scotiae" (MS. Cotton Claudius D 6) in *Chronica Monasterii S. Albani*. ed. Henry Thomas Riley (London, 1865), p. 397, note 1.

14. *Foedera*, ed., Thomas Rymer, rev. Adam Clarke and Fred Holborrke (London, 1818), II, 38.

15. Sir William Blackstone, *Commentaries on the Laws of England*, ed. Edward Christian (Portland, 1807), I, 459.

16. "Commendatio Lamentabilis in Transitu Magni Regis Edwardi," *Chronicles of the Reigns of Edward I and Edward II*, ed. William Stubbs, (Rolls Series, 1882-1883), II, 9.

17. The section of *Flores Historiarum* beginning with the events of 1266 and concluding with those of 1326 was written by various monks at Westminster. See Luard's introduction, I, xliii; also *The Collected papers of Thomas Frederick Tout* (Manchester, 1934), II, 289-301. The portion containing the notice of the Princess Eleana's birth may have been written by John of London. Cf. Sir Thomas D. Hardy, *Descriptive Catalogue of Materials Relating to the History of Great Britain and Ireland* (Rolls Series, 1862-1871), III, 325.

18. DNB, xxxvi, 136.

19. "Plantagenet, Family of," DNB, XLV, 398.

20. Thomas Walsingham, *Historia Anglicana*, ed. Henry Thomas Riley (Rolls Series, 1863-1864), I, 117.

21. Blackstone, *op. cit.*, IV, 81, 92.

22. *Biographie Universelle (Michaud) Ancienne et Moderne*, XXVI, 560.

23. *Pearl, Cleanness, Patience, and Sir Gawain*, facsimile reproduction from MS. Cotton Nero A x, folio 37a.

24. Herbert Norris, *Costume & Fashion*, rptd. (London, 1950), II, 280; and James Robinson Planche, *A Cyclopaedia of Costume*, I, 343.

25. Royal MS 15 E6, reproduced in Planche, *op. cit.*, facing p. 294. *Le Livorie des Chaperons*, the use of a hood or other item in a single color was much in favor during the reigns of Edward III and Richard II.

26. *Pearl*, ed. Gordon, p. 56.

27. DNB, xxxvi, 136.

28. DNB, xxxii, 34; Thomas Walsingham, *Ypodygma Neustriae*, ed., Henry Thomas Riley (London, 1876), p. 168.

29. DNB, xxvi, 100.

30. W. W. Greg, MLR, 19 (1924), 227.

31. *The Record Interpreter*, compiled by Charles Trice Martin, 2nd ed., (London: Stevens & Sons, 1919), pp. 66, 154.

32. *Uoc* is used here ironically, probably with *gostliche* inferred.

33. *Foedera*, II, 38.

34. Documents issued "teste rege" on June 16 at Windsor and on June 19 and 22 at Marlborough (Foedera, II, 50-52). See also Charles Henry Hartshorne, *The Itinerary of King Edward the Second* (privately distributed, 1861), p. 2.

35. DNB, XXVI, 100.

36. *Ibid.*, XIV, 413.

37. *Encyclopaedia Britannica* (1948), VI, 759c.

38. Fowler, *History of Beaulieu Abbey*, p. 11. For origin of the name *Schirebourne*, see Eilart Ekwall, *The Concise Oxford Dictionary of English Place-Names*, 2nd ed. (Clarendon Press, 1936; 2nd ed., 1940).

39. Fowler, p. 97.

40. *Pearl*, ed. Gordon, p. 52.

41. Fowler, *idem*.

42. James E. Thorold Rogers, *A History of Agriculture and Prices in England* (Oxford, 1866), I, 288-291.

43. T. F. Tout, *Chapters in the Administrative History of Medieval England* (Manchester, 1920-1933), V, 287-288.

44. DNB, xxxvi, 136.

45. *Ibid.*, XVII, 37-38.

46. Sir James H. Ramsay, *Genesis of Lancaster* (Oxford: Clarendon Press, 1913), I, 9-10, and DNB, XXVI, 100.

47. Sir Frederic Pollock and Frederic William Maitland, *The History of English Law Before the Time of Edward I*, 2nd ed. (Cambridge University Press, 1923), II, 395.

48. Ramsay, *op. cit.*, I, 22-46, 120-127 and DNB, LVI, 148-151.

49. *Ibid.*, I, 154-169, and DNB, XXVI, 100.

50. DNB, XXVI, 100-101, and Ramsay, I, 183-185, 203-209.

51. DNB, *idem*.

52. Fowler, pp. 1-2.

52a. Ginsberg elegantly traces the dramatic role the locale plays in the dialectical exchange between the narrator mired in space and time and the otherworldly Pearl maiden. (Cf. bibliography for citation.)

   Johnson too argues that the Pearl poet uses "the pastoral landscape and imagery" to reflect the dynamic changes in the narrator. She points out that "the narrator begins by seeing things as distinct from one another. His 'spot' of loss, his pearl, his garden, are distinguished from other spots, pearls, and gardens....However, in vision he encounters multiple pearls and a heavenly garden, learning that each thing he sees reflects Christ. He finally learns to recognize Christ in disparate elements" (180).

   Stiller too sees the landscape playing an active, dramatic role in the narrator's transformation: "Since the narrator's rejection of natural beauty is part of his rebellion against God's will, his [final] joy in and acceptance of beauty signifies a partial resolution of his spiritual dilemma" (404).

   Elizabeth Petroff convincingly links the garden thematically to the garden of Eden and the vineyard of the Maiden's parable (190-191).

53. E. J. F., Arnould, "Henry of Lancaster and His Livre des Seintes Medicines," Bulletin of John Rylands Library 21 (1937), 352-386.

54. Karl Julius Holzknecht, *Literary Patronage in the Middle Ages*, (Philadelphia, 1923; rptd. New York: Octagon Books, Inc., 1966), pp. 93-94, note 24.

55. *Idem.*

56. *Ibid.*, p. 88.

CHAPTER X

THE VALUE OF THE *PEARL* TODAY

Medieval religious art, regarded from our standpoint, may seem to lack functional simplicity, balance, artistic selection of detail, even individuality. It may appear to be over-ornamented, and the ornament to be meretricious, nonessential. It may seem to strain too much, even to go beyond good sense, in seeking effects of height, brilliance, splendor. It may contain much that is strange and distorted, and yet even the grotesque elements may become commonplace and repetitious. Thus to a modern critic it may seem that in the Middle Ages "there existed no sense of esthetic values" and that the style of that day called for elaboration for its own sake, "specious ornament," accumulation of detail without purpose.

But this is from our point of view. From the medieval viewpoint the purpose was clear: to show, through all the varied and manifold aspects of reality, God's oneness and to suggest the splendor and glory of eternity. Thus, in the cathedrals, the attempt was made to "include the whole of God's creation, not omitting even the devils who beset men's souls,"[1] to convey an effect of countlessness and diversity, and yet through the organization and consonance of the parts to represent the unity of God's world held together by God's mind. In sculpture and painting and stained glass were represented (1) the Mirror of Nature, that is, God the Creator, in the form of Christ, and all his creation, flora and fauna, trees, flowers, herbs, lions, lambs, and singing birds; (2) the Mirror of Knowledge, that is, all the varied labors of field and farm throughout the year, the seasons, the signs of the Zodiac, the

Seven Liberal Arts as allegorical figures, and every sort of scene representing
the crafts and the sciences; and (3) the Mirror of History, showing the Old
Testament stories represented in vivid detail as prefigurements of Christ's
ministry, the lives of saints, and other historical figures and events.

At Chartres alone there are represented, in stone and in glass, more
than 10,000 figures. Every scene and detail is portrayed with realistic care,
not merely for its own sake, but for its revelation of God.

> The level commonplace of humanity is deftly rendered, the
> daily doings of the forge and field and marketplace, the tugging
> labourer, the merchant with his stuffs, the scholar with his
> scrolls. Since the whole and all its visible parts is primarily a
> visible symbol of the unseen and divine power, these humble
> elements had part in its unutterable mystery, and were likewise
> symbols.[2]

Just as the picture details are symbolic, so also are the structural parts
of the cathedral, the shape and height of nave and transept, the articles used
in the service of God, and every other thing. The piers seem to strive upward
toward God. The walls cease to be solid and become a lacy fabric of
windows, brilliant with color and light, opening into eternity. And in
medieval times jeweled crosses, glittering shrines, and sacred vessels with
real rubies and emeralds and priceless pearls were there also to speak of the
things of God that do not decay.

The same effects and the same purpose are evident in Dante. In the
Commedia, as in a cathedral, are massed details, a multitude of figures
representing every kind of humanity, pictures of despair, hope, and
blessedness, and all are symbols of God's meaning. As the protagonist of his
story, Dante himself struggled upward toward God, and he uses light and
light-reflecting jewels as symbols of God's being. As Henry Adams points
out, Dante's "special and chosen source of poetic beauty" is light:

> Light everywhere, – in the sky and earth and sea, in the star, the
> flame, the lamp, the gem, – broken in the water, reflected from
> the mirror, transmitted pure through the glass, or colored
> through the edge of the fractured emerald; dimmed in the mist,
> the halo, the deep water; streaming from the rent
> cloud,...flashing in the topaz and the ruby,...mellowed and
> clouding itself in the pearl;...the brighter "nestling" itself in the
> fainter, the purer set off on the less clear, *come perla in bianca*

fronte, – light in the human eye and face, displacing, figuring, or confounded with its expressions....[3]

In the *Pearl* also, the effects and the purpose are similar. Though it portrays only two characters, not a multitude, it nevertheless brings before the reader not only the multitude of heaven – legions of angels, the 144,000 virgins, the whole city of New Jerusalem – but also manifold aspects of life on earth. It pictures vividly the beauty of flowers, orchards, well-watered plains, and harvest fields as well as the manifestations of sin, grief, and rebellion. It deals with the feudal world, the social distinctions based upon birth and chivalric training, gentle manners (264, 281, 421, 632, 717), *cortoisie* (*passim,* especially 432-480), and the knightly virtues such as largesse and franchise (605-612), as well as theological truth and scholastic inquiry. It brings together all its varied materials – down-to-earth human experience, angelology, the mystical lore of gems, one man's divine vision, Biblical interpretation, with much more than can be summarized in this fashion – and unifies them just as it unifies its diverse images of earthly flowering and decay and heavenly hardness and purity.

The poet of the *Pearl* was fascinated by light just as the makers of the cathedrals and Dante were. To him also the light symbolized God and the knowledge of God. At the climax of the poem the picture of the sacrifice of the Lamb is so brilliantly lighted and colored that is suggests comparison with the great apocalyptic scenes in medieval stained glass – even the one in the north rose window of Chartres Cathedral:

> In the central circle, Christ as King is seated on a royal throne, both arms raised, one holding the golden cup of eternal priesthood, the other blessing the world. Two great flambeaux burn beside Him. The four Apocalyptic figures surround and worship Him; and in the concentric circles round the central medallion are the angels and the kings in a blaze of colour, symbolizing the New Jerusalem.[4]

Nevertheless, a world, no longer believing in the mystical unity of all things, is inclined to discount these effects or even to find them repulsive. Henry Adams, responding to the beauty of Chartres, found the art of Chartres to be "very true – as art, at least: so true that everything else shades off into vulgarity," but nevertheless concludes:

We have done with Chartres. For seven hundred years Chartres has seen pilgrims, coming and going more or less like us, and will perhaps see them for another seven hundred years; but we shall see it no more, and can safely leave the Virgin in her majesty, with her three great prophets on either hand, as calm and confident in their strength and in God's providence as they were when Saint Louis was born, but looking down from a deserted heaven, into an empty church, on a dead faith.[5]

The unpleasant side is stated more openly by another man, who felt just as keenly the emotional power of medieval cathedral architecture. "We feel here," said Heine, speaking of a different cathedral, "the lifting up of the spirit and the trampling of the flesh."

The interior...is itself a hollow cross, and we move about there inside the very instrument of martyrdom; the many-colored windows throw their red and green lights on us like drops of blood and pus;...and beneath our feet gravestones and decay, and with the colossal piers the spirit strives upward, painfully tearing itself from the body, which sinks to the ground like a tired garment...these Gothic cathedrals, these huge structures, wrought so airily, so finely, so delicately, so transparently that they might be taken for Brabant lace in marble: then only, one really feels the power of that age which knew how to master even stone, so that it appears to be almost ghostly etherealized, and this most obdurate of materials proclaims Christian spiritualism.[6]

In the same way, and for similar reasons, one may find Dante repulsive. For instance, Goethe, who was ambivalent about Dante, once said he thought "the Inferno abominable, the Purgatorio dubious, and the Paradiso tiresome."[7] Frankl, the great student of Gothic, states the matter thus:

Understanding of Dante is a touchstone for the understanding of Gothic. Anyone who despises Dante and who nevertheless maintains that he loves the Gothic cathedrals probably has not understood the cathedrals – at least not in the way that they were intended in their time. Of course, much of Dante is strange to us, and this is equally true of the cathedrals. They are just as fearful, just as purifying, just as paradisiacal as the three parts of the Divine Comedy. They are just as unbourgeois, extravagant, magnificent, adventurous, fantastic, ambiguous, obscure, and at the same time irradiated and suffused with unaccustomed light.[8]

Likewise a modern reader may find the content of ideas or imagery of the *Pearl* uncongenial or uninteresting.[8a] He may find the form "artificial," the diction strained, the details overdrawn or "conventional." He may consider the picture of heaven ridiculous and the concept of the Beatific Vision absurd. He may be irritated by the idea that the poem has so much hidden behind the veils and may deny the value of such ambiguity or the very existence of the veils or the fact that anything is hidden.

To those who have no belief in medieval religious ideas, what values may be claimed for this kind of art, specifically for the *Pearl*? First we may claim for it beauty if we can agree to define beauty as the complete harmony of all elements and all details in a work of art. Medieval religious art, including the *Pearl*, has this harmony, achieved in a complex pattern, through the use of a multitude of details, many of them seemingly incongruous, brought into unity through their symbolic relationship to the mystic concept of life.

Second, we may claim for this kind of art an appeal to human imagination and emotion. The reader or viewer may feel exhilaration at the technical mastery shown by those who created such art and may find his emotions involved both in the sweep of the work and in its details. The first readers of the *Pearl* did not understand or like its religious ideas, but they responded to its emotional urgency. Later students found other elements that gripped their attention and stimulated their feelings: the religious ideas, multiple levels of meaning, symbolic elements in the portrait of the child in the poem, the mind of the narrator, the complex organization of images and symbols, the portrayal of spiritual truth. The more clearly we identify and define the different elements in the *Pearl*, the greater its imaginative and emotional appeal will probably be.

Third, we may claim for this kind of art an historical importance, for it brings to a sharp focus some of the ideas that controlled the thinking and the creative activity of many men in a long, busy period of human history.

Christianity can be interpreted in many ways, and even the Middle Ages could not maintain one view or one set of views without change. For instance, there were times when the life of monk or nun was generally held to be infinitely preferable to that of other people – was, in fact, the norm of

Christian life. Witness Vincent de Beauvais, writing for the French royal family in the time of St. Louis. And there were other times when the emphasis was on Christian life in the world, and the life of monk and nun stood in eclipse. Witness Aegidius Romanus, writing for the French royal family in the time of St. Louis's son.

Even more dramatic are the swings between Christianity as a religion of love and Christianity as a religion of law. It was Christianity as a religion of love that animated Western Europe in the great days of cathedral building, from 1150 to 1250.

> Before 1200, the Church seems not to have felt the need of appealing habitually to terror; the promise of hope and happiness was enough; even the portal at Autun, which displays a Last Judgment, belonged to Saint Lazarus, the proof and symbol of resurrection...At Chartres [above the west portal, built in the twelfth century] Christ is identified with His Mother, the spirit of love and grace, and His Church is the Church Triumphant.
>
> Not only is fear absent; there is not even a suggestion of pain; there is not a martyr with the symbol of his martyrdom.[9]

After the Albigensian Crusade and the massacre of heretics by the Inquisition, the spirit of religion changed, and by 1300 "every church portal showed Christ not as Savior but as Judge."[10] Dante illustrates the change: in the *Commedia*, his vision beginning on Friday before Easter, 1300, the sufferings of the damned are portrayed with such painful detail that they seem to the modern reader the most vivid scenes of the poem.

On the other hand, consider the *Pearl*: it gives not one word to the stern commandments in the Bible, nor to the sufferings of the damned, nor to the social mission of religion. Even when hell is mentioned, it is only to emphasize the merciful power of the Virgin Mary (442), the glory and joy of heaven (839-840, 1124-1127), and the gift of salvation that Jesus purchased for men.

The *Pearl* was written nearly a half century later than the *Commedia*, but it recaptures the spirit of the cathedral-building days. Perhaps the Black Death, which struck England first in 1348-1349 and again in 1361 and in 1369, had some part in recalling men to the earlier mystical religion; but the return to the old faith was temporary, and the poet of the *Pearl* was conscious of the forces on the other side, for his poem (as shown in Chapter II) indirectly answers some of the critics of the mystic view.

When the *Pearl* was being written, already in the air or soon to appear was the insistence on religion as law that contributed through Wycliff to the Protestant movement; and in 1401, about the time when our existing manuscript of the *Pearl* was being made, the first fire was kindled for the burning of a Wycliffite and the conditions set up for future religious wars.

Perhaps the poet of the *Pearl* was brought up in the mystic faith and never lost it, or perhaps he was influenced by the faith of the man whose story he retold in the poem or by the faith of the patron for whom he wrote. When huge numbers of people die as in the Black Death or in a World War, there may be one tendency swinging the surviving people toward a rebirth of religious faith and an opposite one hurling them toward greater materialism. In such circumstances a poet might well seek to recapture and express the old, consoling faith.

The view presented in the *Pearl* is subject to criticism, both from the religious and the literary standpoint. Conley, for example, denies greatness to the poem "according to the principle that all great art, somberly or smilingly, takes us into the depths of the dark wood, where dwell the Mysteries."

> Pearl takes us only part way in. What is lacking in its vision is supplied us, not unexpectedly, in the unblinking pages of St. Thomas Aquinas. In effect, the passage is both gloss and critique:
>
> ...through God's mercy, temporary blindness [i.e., folly] is directed medicinally to the spiritual welfare of those who are blinded..., [but only] to the predestined, to *whom all things work together unto good* (Rom. viii.28). Therefore, as regards some, their damnation, as Augustine says.[11]

Similarly the charge has been made that the final statement of the *Pearl* constitutes a major flaw.

> The journey of the narrator extends from ignorance to enlightenment...the narrator's last act is a rebellion. His last speech (stanzas 99, 100) is a realization and acceptance. The expectation is fully developed that he will be cast back to earth to enter his period of enlightened travail. Stanza 101, however, has the narrator utter words which properly belong to the completion of that period...Appearing as it does, the 101st

stanza of resolution and reconciliation is gratuitous and facile.[12]

From our point of view the poem may be said to contradict itself.[12a] Echoing Christ's parable in Matthew xiii. 45-46, the child tells the narrator,

I rede þe forsake þe worlde wode
And porchace þy perle maskelles (743-744)

As Fletcher pointed out, this is the counsel of complete renunciation: you must sacrifice all you have to regain your lost innocence and the pearl of eternal life. But, paradoxically, as it turns out at the end of the poem, you don't have to do anything of the sort. Everything is all right without such drastic action. As the narrator says:

To pay þe Prince oþer sete saȝte
Hit is ful eþe to þe god Krystyin;...(1201-1202)

How can this be? The answer is the faith of the mystic – the belief that the Church through its sacraments offers us the means to eternal life:

> By the fulfilment of certain conditions the devout Christian can attain with certainty to the enjoyment of an abundant measure of grace, sufficient or more than sufficient for all his needs. The effects of prayer and of the sacraments are certain, and are within the reach of all who choose to make use of these means of spiritual advancement. Moreover, the rational appreciation of the mysteries of the Christian faith is open to all, independently of natural ability or acquired skill; they offer an abundantly sufficient field to the reason and imagination of all men, whether lettered or unlettered, whether intellectually acute or dull; they adapt themselves, like the objects of universal desire in the life of the senses, to the capacity of each separate individual.[13]

One of the highest of literary values is the self-enclosed wholeness or completeness that permits a literary work to outlast the civilization that produced it and to carry the life and meaning of a dead period into the life and thinking of persons who live centuries or millenniums later. The *Iliad* has this quality: it contains within itself everything that is needed to make the setting, the actions, the words, thoughts, and manner of life of its characters understandable and real to a reader whose civilization is different in uncounted ways. Likewise the *Aeneid* has it. One reads the *Aeneid* and comes to an understanding of the Roman temperament and way of life that he might never reach otherwise. Perhaps the *Pearl* has this quality

Considering its history – the confusion, controversy, and counter-claims – such an assertion may seem strange or absurd. And yet look at the poem from the various standpoints proposed in the preceding chapters, and see how much is revealed by the poem itself through its own words in spite of the silence of six hundred years.

Matthew Arnold divided art into two kinds: that which treats the world "according to the demand of the senses," and that which treats it "according to the demands of the heart and imagination." Medieval religious art treated life according to the demands of the heart and imagination, but sought to guide the mind in that direction by claiming that the truth of the heart and imagination is really the secret, inner meaning that gives sense and life to the world seen by the senses. The *Pearl* follows that pattern: it asserts, dramatically and imaginatively, man's need to reconcile life and death, to discover the spiritual basis for material existence, and to find again his dead loved ones. But it does more than merely assert the medieval faith: it shows one man's revealing experience so fully and completely that the strangeness of the medieval way of thought seems to drop away and we see a human being and participate in a real human experience.

The Middle Ages are a long way from us, and some of us may still feel, as Henry Adams said, a "deep distrust" of everyone who lived in them or believes in them. We may limit our idea of a heavenly vision to some joke about what St. Peter said to the used-car salesman, and we may stand aghast at the ridiculous idea of a heaven devoted to marching and singing, with the sight of God's face a sufficient intellectual occupation for eternity. Nevertheless the Age of Faith once existed, and the people who lived then had hearts and minds and needs like ours and they contributed to making us what we are. For our own sake we need to understand them, and the only way is through the art they left us.

Reading the *Pearl* brings a sort of illumination. We feel suddenly a leap of understanding: we grasp for a moment a little of the meaning of the Age of Faith. We feel the sense of wonder and mystery: the simultaneity of heaven and our world comes home to us, the sense of vast timelessness enclosing our tightly clocked world, the wonder of a divine love that created for us both this earth and a heavenly city. In the light of the *Pearl* we understand a little of what Hugh of St. Victor meant when he wrote:

> He who believes that this world was made for his sake will not look for the reason of it outside of himself. For all was made in the image of the world within him; the earth which is below, is the sensual nature of man, and the heaven above it the purity of his intelligence quickening to immortal life.[14]

And for a moment if no more, the Middle Ages cease to be strange and become a part of our understanding.

Chapter X
Endnotes

1. Taylor, *The Medieval Mind*, II, 109.

2. *Ibid.*, II, 111-112.

3. Henry Adams, *Mont-Saint-Michel and Chartres*, with introduction by Ralph Adams Cram (Boston: Houghton Mifflin, 1933), pp. 185-186.

4. *Ibid.*, p. 195.

5. Paul Frankl, *The Gothic: Literary Sources and Interpretations through Eight Centuries* (Princeton University Press, 1960), p. 478.

6. *Ibid.*, p. 225.

7. Henry Adams, *op. cit.*, p. 70.

8. *Idem.*

8a. Such an attitude is exemplified by W. A. Davenport who finds the poem lacking in emotional unity– "The poem begins and ends with high poetry and strong feeling; between the two peaks lies a tract of stony ground, the enclosed 'intellectual' portion of the poem which is, in parts, prosaically presented and rigid in effect" (50) and in similar vein: "Form and symbolism work at the level of the reader's perception of a complete movement around a moral circle; narrative and feeling work at the level of the Dreamer's confusion" (54).

   Davenport's assumption that there is a division between "stony" doctrine and the "peaks" of affective experience tends to underestimate the genuine power and force of the poem's doctrinal underpinning. Such a reading imposes modern preconception upon a medieval text.

9. John Allen Conley, *loc. cit.*, p. 347.

10. Stern, JEGP, 54 (1955), 691.

11. A. B. Sharpe, *Mysticism*, pp. 68-69.

12. *De Sacramentis*, Book I (Migne Patrologia Latina, 176), Prologue, quoted in translation by Taylor, *The Medieval Mind*, II, 94.

12a. Sklute, by contrast, argues that "the last stanza of *Pearl* is successfully realized both thematically and structurally. He points out that the "last stanza...is separated from the rest of the poem by a span of time. In the final statement, the voice of the narrator is clearly different from the voice in previous stanzas....This stanza could be seen as an independent unit serving as a setting in which the perfect roundness of the pearl is placed" (678). Thematically, he argues – between stanzas

100 and 101 the dreamer recognizes "that he did not need to leave the earth to approach [the godhead]. Rather it was present for him in the Eucharist whose essential mystery is its offer of bliss here on Earth" (678-679).

EPILOGUE

The *Pearl*, a story in verse written 600 years ago, came into the modern world like a beautiful and mysterious waif from a long-dead era. Victorian scholars did not understand it, but responded to its emotional power. Modern scholars have written copiously about it, but have never penetrated its core of mystery. Who are the people in the poem? Why are their names withheld? Why does the narrator speak with such urgency and, at the same time, such reticence? What does the poem mean?

The Amazing Medieval Pearl Re-examined presents the results of a long search for answers, which came slowly and haltingly through a series of discoveries:

1. The *Pearl* does not discuss the main ideas presented: it dramatizes them.

2. It was written in conformity with a concept of poetry very different from the modern concept. This must be understood before the *Pearl* can be read with understanding.

3. It was composed in conformity with the prevailing conditions of authorship in the Middle Ages – i.e., it was written for a patron, whose desire for secrecy must be respected and who becomes legal owner of the poem, when finished.

These and other discoveries culminated in the finding of substantial evidence, most of it available all the while, but completely overlooked; namely, veiled allusions in the *Pearl* itself; telltale colors in a crude picture in the only surviving manuscript; a hidden message in two lines of innocent-looking verse; ironic entries in old chronicles of kings and queens and their loves and hates; and a revealing emblem on a fourteenth-century gravestone.

This evidence, presented in detail in Chapter IX, places the *Pearl* in a definite historic context. It identifies the characters. It names the setting.

These identifications touch royalty and tie the *Pearl* to a revelation of love and adultery, hatred, sin and misery, rebellion, death and hopelessness, and finally forgiveness and peace through the grace of God.

The *Pearl*, both by what it says and what it implies, provides a marvelous insight into the greatness and the darkness and cruelty of the medieval era.

It also offers some powerful thoughts for modern readers.

A Personal Note

I first learned of the *Pearl* while a student in high school. I was looking through a textbook of English literary history, and my glance fell on the picture of a haunted-looking man standing over a grave, and I read about a father who spoke of his grief for a lost child with strange beauty by telling of the pearl that had slipped through his fingers and was lost in the grace.

Perle plesauante to Prynces paye ...

There was only the picture, a summary of the poem's content (based on the interpretation current in the early 1900's), and a few lines in an odd spelling I had never seen before, but it was enough to impress the poem on my imagination.

In my sophomore year in college I looked up the *Pearl* in the library but was doubly disappointed. It was Gollancz's edition, with the text and his translation on alternate pages. I couldn't read the original, and the translation seemed awkward, pretentiously poetic, and somehow empty.

In graduate school I chose medieval English language and literature as my field of specialization; and, after I had acquired some skill in reading Middle English, I turned eagerly to the *Pearl* and read it straight through without stopping. My immediate reaction was that it contained many hints and implications that should be investigated and was a far more interesting poem that Gollancz and other Victorial scholars had supposed.

While teaching in college, after completing my graduate work and in spite of a heavy class-load and piles of papers to grade, I resolved to make a thorough study of the *Pearl* and to publish the results. I first went through the poem carefully, word by word, trying to single out and define the implications and hints, and then I tried to read everything that had been written about the *Pearl*. I found a growing number of articles raising questions about the *Pearl* and/or proposing new interpretations. Some seemed far-fetched, but many, I thought, offered valid insights.

In 1948 I made my first effort to write about the *Pearl*. I prepared a paper and read it to a group of colleagues and undergraduates. I had made some discoveries and was excited about them, but my audience were not impressed. They registered more interest in C. S. Lewis's *The Allegory of Love* when one of my colleagues brought up some of Lewis's ideas.

With a sigh I put my paper away, but I could not leave it alone. I came back to it again and again, renewed my research, broadened my study to include medieval history, medieval ideas on religion and philosophy, and the lives and works of predecessors and contemporaries of the *Pearl* poet, including Dante.

Then I wrote another paper. I tried to place my discoveries in clear relation to all that had been written about the *Pearl*, but to avoid controversy. After a long consideration of what I had written and who might be interested in it, I sent the article to *The Review of English Studies* and got this response from one of the editors:

> "Thank you for sending us your article on *Pearl*.
>
> We have read it with interest and considered it very carefully, but I am sorry to say that we are not at all convinced by your argument."

This was an unexpected blow. I had not presented any argument. I had to think a while to see what was involved. What I found in the poem depended on what I saw in the poem. Someone, even a famous scholar and editor, who had always accepted the established scholarly view of the *Pearl*, was not likely to see the things I had seen.

I knew then, and considered the matter sadly, that it would take a book to show what I had looked for and perhaps another book to show what I actually found. And I did not want to spend so much of my life on one poem.

But this mood did not last. I couldn't give up.

The project meant more investigation outside my own field, particularly in medieval social and intellectual history. I found the studies difficult but intriguing.

I wanted to do a small, easy book, but the effort to select, organize, shape, and write proved harrowing and endless. I wrote and discarded hundreds of pages.

In 1961 the University gave me a semester's leave to work on my project, and I devoted a spring and a summer to projecting and writing a complete manuscript. But it was not what I wanted it to be, and I worked on it as much as I could during the rest of the academic year and again in the summer of 1962.

I completed a second draft by the summer of 1963 and took the first chapter with me to Europe. I visited the British Museum and many places of medieval interest – Winchester, Salisbury, Beaulieu, as well as Paris, Chartres, Amiens, and the Loire Valley. I also stopped at Cambridge and left my chapter there to be read by the Syndics of the Press.

After reading it, they told me they would like to see my book, but they did not give me much encouragement.

When I got home, I read my manuscript through and decided I had failed to establish my points. So I did not sent it to Cambridge. Instead, I put it away. Perhaps I was held back partly by a subconscious fear I would be treated as Schofield and Max Garrett had been and might even become an embarrassment to my university.

Late in my retirement I met by chance in the University library a former student of mine, now teaching in the public schools, and he gravely reproached me for not publishing my book on the *Pearl*. I don't remember his exact words, but they touched my conscience.

I went home, dug my manuscript out of a dusty pile of papers in a crowded cabinet, and started reworking it. The reorganizing and rewriting were not easy and took a long time, but somehow in the process I came to make understandable the evidence that proves incontrovertibly the correctness of the new reading.

I completed this book in my eighty-second year.

A Note To Young Scholars

Because my memory and eyesight are failing and because it is not reasonable to expect that the professors now in power, being already committed to the traditional interpretation of the *Pearl*, will accept what I have found, I am counting on you, young scholars of today and tomorrow, to understand, verify, and complete the work I have begun: specifically, to test, evaluate, and, where possible, add to the evidence presented here, particularly that in Chapter IX; to gather additional relevant data on the persons directly or indirectly involved in the story (Edward I, Queen Margaret, Edward II, Queen Isabella, the two Despensers, Thomas and Henry of Lancaster, and the Princess Eleana Margareta); and to investigate further the ideas dramatized in the *Pearl*, the theory and practice of veiled verse, and the use by Dante and the *Pearl* poet of a modified, corrigible form of multi-level meaning.

Eventually, you and others will no doubt sort out all that is valid in previous writings about the *Pearl* and fit each valid part into its place in the framework suggested in this book

Perhaps also your studies will determine whether the author of the *Pearl* was directly influenced by Dante.

I wish I could live to see how it all comes out.

G. D. B.

Southern Methodist University
Dallas, Texas
October, 1985

BIBLIOGRAPHY

Andrew, Malcolm.
  "*Pearl* 161," *Explicator*, vol. 40, no. 1 (Fall 1981): pp. 4-5.

Bogdanos, Theodore.
  Pearl: Image of the Ineffable, A Study in Medieval Poetic Symbolism.
  University Park and London: Pennsylvania State University Press,
  1983.

Carlson, David.
  "The Pearl Poet's Olympia." *Manuscripta* (Nov, 1987): 181-189.

Carroll, Christopher Franklin.
  "The People in *Pearl*: Audience, Poet, Narrator, Dreamer, and
  Maiden." *Dissertation Abstracts International*, 31 (1970): 2336 A.

Chapman, Coolidge Otis.
  "Numerical Symbolism in Dante and the *Pearl*." *Modern Languages
  Notes*, vol. 54, (1930): 256-269.

Davenport, W. A.
  The Art of the Gawain Poet. London: University of London, Athelone
  Press, 1978.

Eldredge, Laurence.
  "The State of *Pearl*: Studies Since 1933." *Viator* 6 (1975): 1-12.

Field, Rosalind.
  "The Heavenly Jerusalem in Pearl." *Modern Language Review* (Jan.
  1986), vol. 81, no. 1, pp. 7-17.

Gatta, John, Jr.
  "Transformation Symbolism and the Liturgy of the Mass in Pearl."
  Modern Philology, 71 (1974): 243-256.

Ginsberg, Warren.
  "Place and Dialectic in *Pearl* and Dante's *Paradiso*." *English Literary
  History* 55, no. 4 (Winter 1988): 731-754.

Hendrix, Howard V.
  "Reasonable Failure: *Pearl* Considered as a Self-Consuming Artifact
  of 'Gostly Porpose.'" *Neuphilogische Mitteilungen*, vol. 86, no. 4
  (1985): 458-466.

Johnson, Lynn Staley.
  The Voice of the Gawain Poet. London: University of Wisconsin
  Press, 1984.

Manes, Christopher.
"A Plum for the *Pearl* Poet." *English Language Notes*, vol. 23, no. 4 (June 1986): 4-6.

Mann, Jill.
"Satisfaction and Payment in Middle English Literature." *Studies in the Age of Chaucer*, vol. 5 (1983): 17-48.

Milroy, James.
"*Pearl*: The Verbal Texture and the Linguistic Theme." *Neophilogus* 55 (1971): 195-208.

Nelson, Cary.
"*Pearl*: The Circle as Figural Space." Pp. 25-53 of *The Incarnate Word: Literature as Verbal Space*. Urbana: University of Illinois Press, 1973.

Nolan, Barbara Frances.
"*Pearl*: A Fourteenth-Century Vision in August." Pp. 156-204 of the *Gothic Visionary Experience*. Princeton: Princeton University Press, 1977.

Olmert, Michael.
"Game Playing, Moral Purpose, and the Structure of *Pearl*." *Chaucer Review*, vol. 21, no. 3 (1987): 383-403.

Olson, Glending.
"'Nawþer Reste ne Travayle': The Psychology of *Pearl*." *Neuphilogische Mitteilungen*, vol. 83, no. 4 (1982): 422-425.

Paul, James Allen.
"Aporia and *Pearl*: Medieval Narrative Irony." *Dissertation Abstracts International* 38 (1977): 3476A.

Peterson, Clifford J.
"*Pearl* and *St. Erkenwald*: Some Evidence for Authorship." *Review of English Studies* (1974): 49-53.

Prior, Sandra Pierson.
"Poet of the Word: Patterns and Imagery of the Apocalypse in the works of the Pearl Poet." *Dissertation Abstracts International*, vol. 46, no. 4 (Oct. 1985): 974A-975A.

Rostvig, Maren-Sofie.
"Numerical Composition in *Pearl*: A Theory." *English Studies* 48 (1967): 326-332.

Russell, J. Stephen.
"*Pearl's* Courtesy: A Critique of Eschatology." *Renascence*, vol. 35, no. 3 (1983): 183-195.

Schotter, Howland Anne.
"Vernacular Style and the Word of God: The Incarnational Art of *Pearl*," Pp. 23-32 of *Ineffability: Naming the Unnameable from Dante to Beckett*. Ed. by Peter S. Hawkins and Anne Howland Schotter. New York: AMS Press, 1984.

Sklute, Larry M.
"Expectation and Fulfillment in *Pearl*." *Philological Quarterly* 52 (1973): 663-679.

Stiller, Nikki.
"The Transformation of the Physical in The Middle English *Pearl*." *English Studies*, vol. 63, no. 5 (October 1982): 402-409.

Watts, Ann Chalmers.
"*Pearl*, Inexpressibility, and Poems of Human Loss." *PMLA* 99, no. 1 (Jan. 1984): 26-40.

Wilson, Edward.
"Word Play and the Interpretation of *Pearl*." *Medium Aevum* 40 (1971): 116-134.

INDEX

STUDIES IN MEDIAEVAL LITERATURE